W0017224

HOPE AMID HARDSHIP

Pioneer Voices from Kansas Territory

Edited and illustrated by Linda S. Johnston

With Compliments
Weider History Group
www.historynet.com

TWODOT®

Guilford, Connecticut
Helena, Montana
An imprint of Globe Pequot Press

A · T W O D O T® · B O O K

TwoDot is an imprint of Globe Pequot Press and a registered trademark of Morris Book
Publishing, LLC.

All illustrations by Linda S. Johnston.

Project editor: Meredith Dias
Text design: Sheryl P. Kober
Layout: Sue Murray

Library of Congress Cataloging-in-Publication Data

Johnston, Linda S.
  Hope amid hardship : pioneer voices from Kansas Territory / edited by
Linda S. Johnston.
     pages cm
  Includes bibliographical references.
  ISBN 978-0-7627-8486-8
  1. Kansas—History—1854–1861. 2. Pioneers—Kansas—Biography. 3.
Pioneers—Kansas—Correspondence. 4. Frontier and pioneer life—Kansas.
I. Title.
  F685.J76 2013
  978.1'02—dc23
                                        2013015001

Printed in the United States of America

10 9 8 7 6 5 4 3 2 1

To my mom,
a pioneer in her own right.

CONTENTS

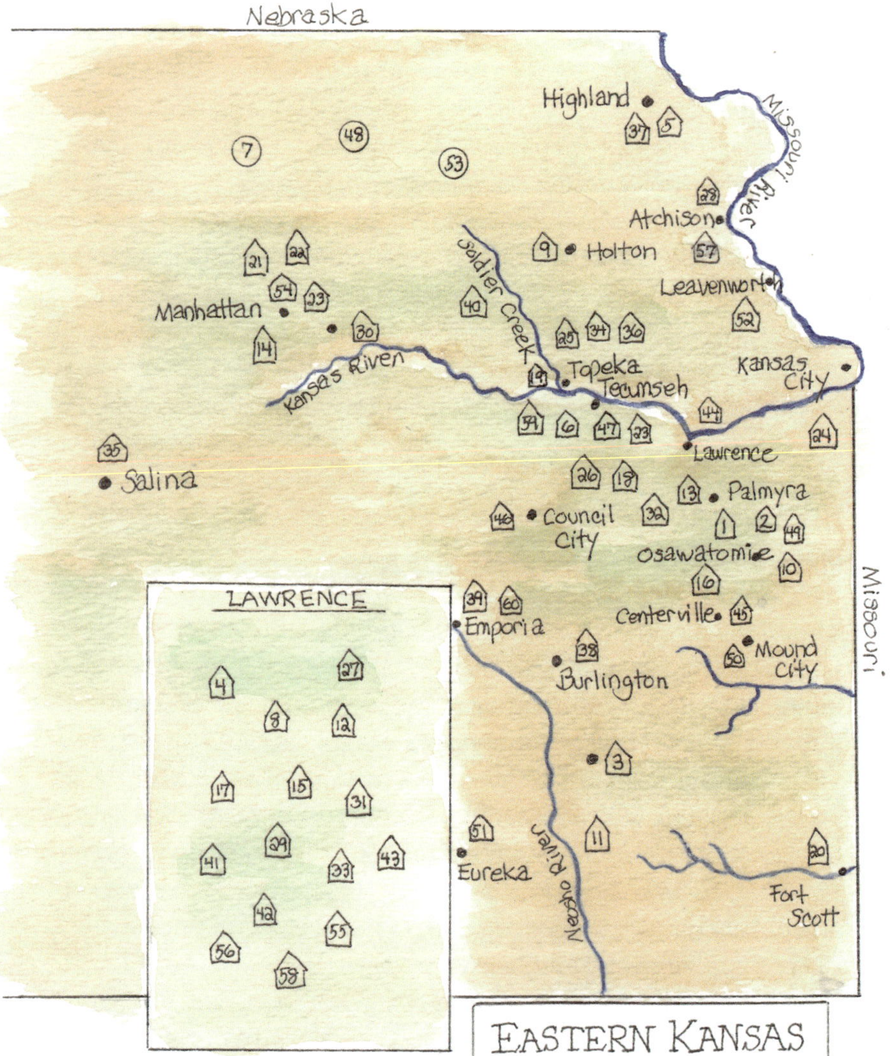
Nebraska
Highland
37
5
7
48
53
28
Atchison
9
Holton
57
Missouri River
Leavenworth
52
21
22
54
23
Manhattan
30
14
40
Soldier Creek
25
34
36
Kansas River
19
Topeka
Tecumseh
Kansas City
44
59
6
47
23
24
Lawrence
35
Salina
26
18
13
Palmyra
46
Council City
32
1
2
49
Osawatomie
10
16
Missouri
LAWRENCE
4
27
8
12
17
15
31
29
41
33
43
42
55
56
58
39
60
Emporia
Centerville
45
38
Burlington
50
Mound City
3
51
Eureka
Neosho River
11
20
Fort Scott

EASTERN KANSAS TERRITORY

1. Adair, Samuel
2. Allen, Chestina Bowker
3. Anderson, Melissa Genett
4. Bacon, L.S.
5. Bayless, John
6. Bourassa, Joseph (Ke Kahn)
7. Boynton, C.B.
8. Brown, John Stillman
9. Bryant, Peter
10. Carruth, Jane & Lucy
11. Colt, Miriam
12. Cordley, Richard
13. Deering, John Henry
14. Denison, Henry
15. Elliott, Robert Gaston
16. Everett, John & Sarah
17. Fitch, Edward
18. Gilbert, Robert S.
19. Giles, F.W.
20. Goodlander, Charles W.
21. Goodnow, Isaac & Ellen
22. Goodnow, William
23. Griffing, James
24. Hildt, George
25. Holliday, Cyrus K.
26. Hoole, A.J.
27. Hubbell, Willard Orvis
28. Ingalls, John J.
29. Leamard, Oscar E.
30. Lines, Charles B.
31. Litchfield, Timothy Lewis
32. Lovejoy, Julia Louisa
33. Mayo, Thankful & Frank
34. McVicar, Peter
35. Mead, James R.
36. Miller, Joseph C.
37. Minion, Mrs. C.J.
38. Puffer, Charles
39. Randolph, Anna Margaret
40. Reader, Samuel J.
41. Robinson, Sara
42. Ropes, Hannah Anderson
43. Savage, Joseph
44. Sears, Mary
45. Sessions, Moses C.
46. Stewart, James R.
47. Stinson, Thomas N.
48. Tomlinson, William
49. Tovey, Robert Atkins
50. Trego, Joseph H.
51. Tucker, Edwin
52. Valentine, Daniel Mulford
53. George Walter
54. Wells, Thomas
55. Whitney, E.S.
56. Wilmarth, George
57. Woods, Walter Hastings
58. Herald of Freedom
59. Kansas Tribune
60. Kanzas News

ACKNOWLEDGMENTS

This project has given me the chance to learn, to appreciate, and to grow, and for that I am truly fortunate. To acknowledge all of those who have helped me during this twenty-five-year project would be a monumental task. First, thank you to Erin Turner, my editor at TwoDot and a fellow baseball fan, for seeing the potential in this project, and for her approval of the exclamation point!

Thanks also to Meredith Dias, project editor, and Melissa Hayes, copy editor, for their expert care in polishing the manuscript.

My appreciation goes to Lin Fredericksen and the research staff at the Kansas Historical Society. Their expertise and helpfulness is boundless. For answering numerous questions in person and through e-mail, thank you to Theresa Coble, Susan Forbes, Debbie Greeson, and Sara Keckeisen.

I would also like to thank the librarians, archivists, and researchers who collaborated to create Territorial Kansas Online, an invaluable resource on early Kansas.

My research was funded in part by an Edward N. Tihen Historical Research Grant administered by the Kansas Historical Foundation. This generous award helped make my final research trip to Kansas possible. Thank you so very much to Terry Marmet and Vicky Henley from the Foundation for their assistance and kindness.

The Spencer Research Library at the University of Kansas houses a wonderful collection of diaries and other materials from early Kansas. Thank you to the research staff for their assistance. Also at the University of Kansas, Craig Freeman and Caleb Morse from the Ronald L. McGregor Herbarium provided help identifying native plants. Special appreciation goes to Craig for nomenclature assistance.

William Griffing was kind enough to share stories of his great-great-grandparents, James and Augusta Griffing. Thank you to him, especially for the story of the Griffings' friendship with Thomas and Ella Wells.

Many of the writers in this book wrote about farming, something I know little about. For information on making hay, I turned to my dear friend, Jeannie Heflin, and her husband Carl.

I would like to give special acknowledgment to Women Writing the West, Virginia Writers Club, and Write by the Rails, writing organizations that educate, encourage, nourish, and inspire. In these groups I have met kind and generous people and made many friends.

Writing teachers often remind students to show, not tell. This project would not have been possible had it not been for the original writers of the West, the pioneers who showed me the meaning of hope amid hardship.

This will be the only time my family comes last. Thank you to Chris for computer assistance, and to Jen for thoughtful help with drafts of the text and map. My husband, Clay, has been there to do whatever needed to be done, including typing and making sure I had everything I needed during the long days at the computer. My daughter, Sarah, and son, Andrew, rode in the backseat to dozens of historic sites over the years, and are still the most interesting traveling companions a person could ever have. Along with Clay, they have always cheered me on, and that has made all the difference.

INTRODUCTION

I think you would be enraptured with the splendid wild flowers, as well as the country and if it becomes a free state, and our city worthy of you, we shall some day have you for a neighbor. But what you gain there will not more than balance the novelty, and excitement of our new pioneer life which is not so despisable after all. I assure you we have our joys as well as sorrows.

Ellen Goodnow to her sister Harriet
May 18, 1856

Between 1855 and 1860, over 98,000 people settled in Kansas Territory. In a new land fraught with incredible challenges, why did they stay? This question planted a seed that would grow into a lifelong passion for me. My own love affair with Kansas began on the Santa Fe Trail in 1986. I had lived in the Sunflower State for a year, and while my daughter, Sarah, attended preschool, my two-year-old son, Andrew, and I set out on a small adventure each week. One such outing took us southwest from Kansas City to Olathe and a small farm that served as a stagecoach stop on the Santa Fe Trail. The colorful history of the Mahaffie Farmstead fascinated me, and I became a docent a few weeks after that first visit. One day as I waited in the parlor for the next tour group to arrive, a dusty pink book on the shelf caught my attention. I opened Marian Russell's memoirs and read the first page.

"Life has dealt me adventure with a lavish hand and yet the way stretches very fair behind me," she wrote. "It is the brightness, not the darkness that I see as I look backward." Marian, who made five round-trips on the Santa Fe Trail beginning in 1852, described the "miles and miles of buffalo grass, blue lagoons, and blood-red sunsets and, once in a while, a little sod house on the lonely prairie."

Marian's impressions of her trips along the trail captivated me. At that moment I decided to learn more about the men and women who left comfortable homes, friends, and families in places like New York and Massachusetts to settle in a land they knew little about. Already enamored with Kansas, I chose to focus my research on the years 1855 through 1860, the Territorial Era. I did research during the kids' preschool and nap times. Algeline Ashley, on her way across the plains in 1852, scribed, "I write in my lap with the wind rocking the wagon." If she could manage to write in those conditions, I could find the time to read. What called individuals to go west? How did they face the challenges of their new life? And, most important to me, how did they keep their spirits up in times of despair? Anxious to find the answers, I kept reading. As I did, I realized why I felt a kinship with these men and women who had left the familiar for the unknown. With Kansas being number fifteen on my list of residences, I knew about saying good-bye. To help ease the sadness of moving, I thought of each destination as an adventure, an opportunity to make new friends, see new places. Surely the same feelings of possibility filled the hearts of many emigrants as they started for Kansas Territory. Although separated by more than a century, these pioneers and I shared loss and hope, apprehension and anticipation, weariness and excitement—the emotions of packing up and settling down.

During the next fifteen years, job relocations took our family from Kansas to Virginia, on to Chicago and back to Virginia, but I never really left Kansas behind. I researched when I could, including trips to the Library of Congress in Washington, D.C. My daughter went on to attend the University of Kansas, and my visits there included time at the Spencer Research Library and at the Kansas Historical Society in Topeka. As we walked on the beautiful campus atop Mount Oread,

I thought about Charles and Sara Robinson, who lived there and later donated the land to the University. We shopped along Massachusetts Avenue, where Joseph Savage and the first group of Lawrence settlers camped on their first night in the Territory in the autumn of 1854, and where the first Fourth of July parade took place in 1855.

Finally, in 2006, I began to organize my years of Kansas research into a book. With my goal to present historical material in a personal way, I decided to include watercolor sketches and newspaper items to provide some additional context. I reviewed each person's writings. Like dear friends who have been parted for a time, the settlers and I took up just where we'd left off, with Edward Fitch playing in the Lawrence Band, John Deering playing cards and singing with friends, and Sarah Everett describing prairie wildflowers. When I came across a diary that I hadn't discovered previously, it was like meeting someone new. Occasionally I realized that two or three of the writers had been at the same wedding or picnic and must have known each other. As this happened, the communities seemed to reemerge. The word *hope* began to catch my eye as I read. I began a tally. When the "hope count" had reached fifty, I knew I'd found the essence of the project. Hope—the invisible compass point that even in the dark helps one to see the way ahead. Charles Lines, who came to the Territory from Connecticut in 1856, captured the importance of hope in a letter to the New Haven, Connecticut, *Daily Palladium:*

> *Hope is a powerful stimulus in all our migrations and trials in this world, and we feel its blessed influence here. We are content, though absent from those we dearly love, because we are still joined in heart and hope to meet again. And we rejoice notwithstanding our deprivations, because we hope "there is a good time coming," and we are willing to "wait a little longer." It is more and more wonderful to us every succeeding day to notice how pioneers live, and yet how content they seem.*

Settlers needed everything they could muster—hope, courage, and patience—to meet the challenges of their adopted home. The political climate posed just such a challenge. On May 26, 1854, Congress passed the Kansas–Nebraska Act. Although the slavery issue had already invoked passionate discussion across the country, the signing of the bill crystallized sentiments and brought Kansas into sharp focus. The legislation created the Kansas and Nebraska Territories from the northern section of the Louisiana Purchase. Additionally, the bill repealed the ban on slavery put in place by the 1820 Missouri Compromise, and left it for the residents of the territories to decide whether or not to allow slavery. An emotional, divisive, and often violent conflict, the slavery question remained a part of life in Kansas until the Territory joined the Union as the thirty-fourth state on January 29, 1861.

With the passage of the Kansas–Nebraska Act, Kansas opened her prairies to the world. Settlers came from as far away as Germany and as near as Missouri. Emigrants came by train, steamboat, stagecoach, and wagon, or a combination thereof. Many Northerners traveled with organized groups, such as the New England Emigrant Aid Company, founded specifically to populate the new territory with settlers of antislavery sentiment. Once in Kansas, a person's place of origin made little difference, as Woodson County pioneer Melissa Genett Anderson wrote:

> And we had good neighbors all around. It made no difference whether they were Yanks, Buckeyes, Hoosiers, Missourians, or what not – we were neighbors. And we all used the English language, even if our expressions were some times different.

Music, a language everyone understood, lightened the mood in the Territory, whether it came from George Hildt singing alone on the prairie, or from the Lawrence Band playing at a social event. Holidays, weddings, and parties—these were the times when burdens were lighter, the occasions that gave settlers reason to sing, dance, and celebrate. Eager to socialize, settlers organized literary groups and worshipped together. They found comfort in familiar music and traditions, and in each other's company. During quiet moments, they filled diaries and letters with wonderful descriptions of these events, and of the natural world around them, including spring and summer wildflowers.

Words and images preserve a moment, day, or event, and become part of our historical fabric. As Willa Cather wrote in *O, Pioneers!*, "The history of every country begins in the heart of a man or a woman." *Hope Amid Hardship* is a look into the hearts of sixty men and women who settled in early Kansas and recorded their joys, fears, and observations. No matter the circumstances, they took pen in hand to write about their experiences, as Chestina Bowker Allen did on a snowy day in March 1855, when she noted, "The snow falls upon my book while I write by the stove." This collection of writings illustrates the importance of the written personal record, not only of the celebrated figures who make history, but also of the everyday men and women whose contributions often go unnoticed.

Why did they stay? Perhaps Mary Sears, who intended to stop in Kansas only for a few days but stayed for more than twenty-five years, helped answer the question in her recollections when she wrote, "True, the pioneer days were often lonely and wearisome, and yet somehow we found the spirit of happiness. The very isolation developed among us a sense and service of helpfulness one to the other."

I hope these writers would be pleased to know that so many years later, others can see the brighter side of pioneer life, illuminated by their words. It is my privilege to introduce these fascinating individuals, who after so many years feel to me like dear friends whose journeys have become part of my own.

Note: The extracts from the diaries, letters, and newspaper items are presented as they were originally written. To preserve the character of the writings, no changes have been made to spelling, grammar, or punctuation.

Spring

This is a most lovely day. Hope is lightening up the hearts of the settlers. The spring rains are giving way to bright and lovely weather, and summer-time is coming with its beautiful array of lovely, bright-eyed flowers.

Miriam Colt
Neosho River, West of Fort Scott
May 24, 1856

Buds on the cottonwood trees burst open. Wildflowers brought color back to the face of the prairie with blue, yellow, and violet. As the landscape around them came back to life, many Kansas settlers, including Sarah Everett and Miriam Colt, described the sight in their letters and journals. Familiar flowers provided a comforting connection between new home and old, and something tangible to describe in letters to loved ones and friends.

With the ground thawed and their spirits renewed, settlers began plowing fields and planting corn, oats, and wheat. Vegetable gardens and fruit orchards took shape, thanks, in part, to parcels of seeds and cuttings sent from family and friends in the East. Some newcomers farmed for the first time and received help from neighbors. James Stewart learned from neighbor Prentiss, "who came up with his team and broke prairie for me, myself holding the plow . . .

this is the first of my Prairie farming . . ." Edward Fitch wrote to his father, "I suppose you are having cold weather there now but we are having fine spring like weather tho today is cloudy. Folks are plowing some and things begin to look like spring. . . ."

As wheat and wildflowers took root, so did new towns with names like Sugar Mound, Kickapoo City, and Grasshopper Falls. Emigrants traveled by train, steamboat, and wagon to try a different way of life. In an 1855 letter to the editor of the New Hampshire *Independent Democrat*, Julia Louisa Lovejoy, one of the first citizens of Manhattan, wrote: "towns are starting up as by magic all along the valley of the Kanz[a]s." Guides, such as Edward E. Hale's *Kanzas and Nebraska*, considered to be the first book on Kansas, gave prospective settlers information on routes, weather, and landscape. Hale's book, as well as others, such as J. Butler Chapman's *History of Kansas and Emigrant's Guide* (1855), also included news of the political situation.

The Kansas–Nebraska Act of 1854 put a national focus on the Kansas Territory, and in particular, the status of Kansas (free or slave state) when it entered the Union. The slavery question caused much controversy in the Territory. The political strife often resulted in violence, including the "Sack of Lawrence" in May 1856, when several buildings were destroyed, including those housing the two free-state newspapers. Although the slavery issue did encourage many people to emigrate for a moral cause, many others came for more practical reasons. Kansas meant opportunities, business and personal. Coming from as near as Iowa and as far away as Germany, new citizens came with diverse skills and trades that would develop commerce and build communities. John Deering opened a wagon shop in Prairie City. Joseph Trego operated a sawmill on Little Sugar Creek in Linn County. In 1859, *Barclay's Business Directory of Leavenworth*, the largest city in the Territory, listed 500 businesses, including shoemakers, sign painters, and booksellers.

When not working at their trades or on their farms, settlers enjoyed each other's company at social events such as dances and parties, where the Lawrence Band, also known as the Lawrence Cornet Band, often played. Newspapers featured items on dramatic presentations. In his diary, Willard Hubbell mentioned going to "the Lodge." Fraternal organizations such as the Independent Order of Good Templars of Kansas, the International Order of Odd Fellows, and the Ancient Order of Accepted Masons had lodges in Lawrence, Tecumseh, and Leavenworth. A walk or wagon ride to a neighbor's claim or into town provided a chance to visit, purchase supplies, and pick up mail. Some settlers used their free time to play music or read letters and newspapers from home. A few minutes at the end of the day provided time to answer letters from family or catch up in one's diary.

James Rogers, who came to Kansas in 1856, described the social side of territorial life this way:

> . . . you must remember, that every cloud has its silver lining, and that all these dark days were compensated in a measure, by the equality, sociability and friendship which must result from such a state of affairs . . . Then were frequent picnics, sociables, festivals - aye bachelor's festivals even, surprises and excursions; and in short we all lived like neighbors.

Although neighbors on the prairie might be miles apart, occasionally a few would get together and drive one or two wagons to the house of another settler and the party would begin, much to the surprise of the chosen host and hostess. More formal events took place at larger halls or hotels, such as the Eldridge House in Lawrence. On May 21, 1858, the hotel was the site of a ball, the proceeds going to the fire department.

Religion played an important role in the life of many early Kansans. On a personal level, faith provided comfort and a source of strength during difficult times. In the community, the Sabbath meant a time to come together for worship, whether in a log cabin, where Thomas Wells wrote that the Methodists met, or in the Masonic Hall, where Lawrence Baptists gathered. Several religious denominations had an early presence in Kansas Territory. The Methodist Church supported communities in another important way, by founding and supporting two of the first colleges: Bluemont College in Manhattan, which later became Kansas State University, and Baker University in Baldwin City. These institutions not only brought teachers and students to the area, but prestige as well.

Springtime in the Territory meant new beginnings—building a home, a town, a new life—none of them easy tasks. As the writers' words reveal, even on a day filled with hard work, there could be time for pleasure.

Emigration

In April 1857, twenty-year-old Edwin Tucker left Beloit, Wisconsin, for Kansas Territory. His father David and uncle Elijah traveled with him. The three helped found Eureka, located in present Greenwood County.

Edwin Tucker, considered by his community to be a generous and sympathetic man, contributed to Eureka and Kansas through the many roles he took on. As a successful cattleman, landowner, and banker, he played a major role in the growth of Eureka. In 1858, he organized and taught in the first neighborhood school. His commitment to others continued when he helped residents during the drought of 1860 and the grasshopper plague in 1874. On the state level, he served as a member of the Kansas legislature and a regent of Washburn College.

Edwin married Amelia Willis, another Eureka pioneer, in 1863. The family grew to include seven children, many of whom remained in the area, continuing their father's legacy of community service. Edwin Tucker died on his farm near Eureka in 1911.

In his diary, Edwin described the scene as he left Beloit in the spring of 1857:

Thurs April 16, 1857
We bid goodbye to friends this morning and started for Kansas; our enthusiasm for Kansas could not quite drown our feelings of sadness at parting from relatives, friends, home and nearly all, which is dear on earth. We hardly know what it is to leave home until we learn by experience. Neighbors gathered and helped us start . . .

Thankful Sophia Cobb and Frank Mayo married in Massachusetts in the early 1850s. The two decided to emigrate to Kansas, Frank traveling with the second party of the New England Emigrant Aid Society in 1855, Thankful set to join him later. Frank built a house on his claim south of Lawrence and waited for his wife, who arrived in September 1855.

During their three years in Lawrence, the Mayos had a son, Elisha Cobb Mayo. Frank, Thankful, and their son returned to Massachusetts in 1858, and shortly after, a daughter, Rebecca,

joined the little family. Sadly, Frank died soon after his daughter was born, and Thankful never returned to their Kansas home. She married Solomon Harris in 1863, and in 1880, after Solomon's death, moved to Sonoma, California, with her son and daughter.

Thankful's journal intertwines diary entries about the day Frank left for the Territory, contents of letters between her and Frank, and their time in Kansas, as she remembered it years later. Writing about her husband's departure (he went to Kansas six months before she did), she described the scene at the Fitchburg Depot:

> *At the depot there was singing–verses composed for the occasion and to the tune of Nelly Bly. . . .*

Thankful recalled the chorus and continued:

> *Ho Brothers, Ho Brothers, come along with me.*
> *We'll sing upon the Kansas Plains the songs of liberty*

. . . When the bell rang, the crowd sent up a loud huzza. That parting seemed as if I could not bear it! I have learned since how much the heart can bear and yet wearily beat on. . . .

Frank sent words of encouragement to Thankful through the spring and summer to lift her spirits until her arrival in September 1855:

May 5th 1855
Lawrence, Kansas Territory
Cheer up! Thanky, keep up a stout heart as you tell me. The darkest time is just before day . . .

June 10th 1855
Dear Thanky keep up good courage take good care of your health you will soon be with me.

August, 1855
Keep up good courage Thanky when you are on your way out. Remember that your husband is ahead of you. He has traveled the road all over before you (cannot fear the valley of the shadow which he has traveled before me. Ah! He is ahead of me in the land of spirits and my way is long). Fear not, my beloved wife, I shall meet you in Kansas City . . .

Referring to the journey to Kansas with a group of fellow Rhode Islanders, Joseph C. Miller wrote in his diary, ". . . we embarked on board the cars, and submitted our lives and fortunes to him who held the reins of the iron horse." Miller, a tinsmith by trade, left Boston on March 13, 1855, and arrived in Kansas City on March 24. In documenting the trip and his first several months in Topeka, Miller painted a detailed picture of people, scenery, and events, including his visit to a Kaw Indian camp. He opened the first tin shop and hardware store in Topeka. An integral part of the community, he belonged to the Baptist Church and served as justice of the peace. In June 1855, Miller and his wife, Sarah, enjoyed a long-anticipated reunion when she arrived in Topeka. The couple had four children. Joseph died in Topeka in 1879. In his diary, Joseph described the scene as he left for the Territory:

Boston March the 13th/55
A company of about two hundred started from Boston this day
en route for Kansas, which lay in the far west; a land which had
by common report become known and hailed as the garden of
America; a land of the richness of which was not to be surpassed
by any on the globe, and a land the beauty of whose scenery was
not to be excelled even by Italy's sunny clime, among our party
were some going forth to repair a broken fortune, others as seekers
of pleasure . . .

Miller goes on, telling about the passengers:

There was the child of infantile years, the impetuous youth, the
Woman in the prime of life, and the hoary Headed man, all of
whom were seeking the same goal, a home in the far off west and
all of whom I trust were impelled by a higher and holier motive
than mere sordid gain, a desire to make that vast country a home
of the free as well as the brave, to rescue that virgin soil from
becoming polluted with the foul stain of American slavery, and to
preserve its rolling hills and vales from resounding with the echo
of the task masters lash as it is applied to the back of the bond
man. . . .

From the age of five, when she knelt and asked God to "make her a good child," Julia Louisa Lovejoy lived a devout and penitent Christian life, as evidenced in her thirty years of diary entries.

Julia, her husband, Reverend Charles Lovejoy, and their three children, Charles Julius (age seventeen), Juliette (fifteen), and Edith (six), arrived in Kansas City, Missouri, in March 1855. Charles and his son went ahead to find a place for the family to settle. Almost immediately, Julia and her daughters became ill, little Edith coming down with the measles. Circumstances became unbearable, with sickness and deaths increasing in the city. Julia wrote, ". . . if we stay here I fear we shall die."

She and the children boarded a boat to go upriver to Fort Riley, to try to improve their situation, but the boat struck a sandbar only four miles from Kansas City. Edith grew sicker. Julia then hired a man to take them to the Big Blue River, where her husband worked with others to lay out the town that would later become Manhattan. After a harrowing journey, the family reunited, but little Edith died a day later. The loss overshadowed what might otherwise have been joyful news: Julia was six months pregnant. Irving Lovejoy entered the world in September 1855, as the first white child born within the Manhattan city limits.

During his early years in the Territory, Charles Lovejoy served as a traveling preacher in the Manhattan area. Entries in Julia's diary indicate that they also lived in Sumner, Leavenworth, Lawrence, and Palmyra at various times. Several settlers mention Reverend Lovejoy in their diaries and letters.

In October 1860, Julia and Charles's second daughter, Juliette, died at the age of twenty. Three years passed before Julia's next diary entry. Living in Corinth, Mississippi, where her husband served as chaplain of the Seventh Kansas Cavalry, Julia explained the three-year gap that followed their daughter's death: "I have had no heart to write concerning any matter." Her life continued to be one of personal sacrifice, challenge, and sorrow. Julia and Charles later returned to the family farm near Baldwin City, where Julia died in 1882 at age seventy. Charles remained in Douglas County until his death in 1904, at the age of ninety-two.

In 1855, though burdened by the recent death of her young daughter, Edith, Julia found cheerful words to describe her new home near the mouth of the Big Blue River in one of several letters written to the editors of the Concord, New Hampshire, *Independent Democrat:*

> *Mouth of the Big Blue River, K. T.*
> *May 22d, 1855.*
>
> *Mr. Editor:-*
> *We arrived at our intended home about two weeks ago, and,*
> *notwithstanding the vacant spot in the home circle, and our*
> *own desolate hearts, we must pronounce this the most charming*
> *country our eyes ever beheld! I wish to write to our New England*
> *friends, things as we view them in this Territory, and only as far as*
> *we do know them! It seems to us impossible that any spot on earth,*
> *uncultivated by art, can be more inviting in appearance than this*
> *country. . . .*
> *Yours respectfully,*
> *Julia Louisa Lovejoy*

In 1849, Sara Tappan Doolittle Lawrence, a well-educated young woman from a prominent Massachusetts family, met Charles Robinson, a physician in Fitchburg, Massachusetts. The two married in October 1851. Both Charles and Sara held abolitionist views, and soon after hearing of the Kansas–Nebraska Act and the New England Emigrant Aid Company, decided on a move to the Kansas Territory. In 1854, Charles, having become an agent for the Company, made two trips to the area, guiding settlers and helping to plan the town. Sara joined him in May 1855.

Due to his strong antislavery views and activities, Charles was arrested in May 1856, and spent time in prison at the pro-slavery capital, Lecompton. Sara remained a free-state supporter, and during her husband's absence, wrote extensively, keeping emigrant aid and congressional leaders informed on the cause and her husband's situation. In 1856, she published *Kansas: Its Interior and Exterior Life*. The book documents the events and sentiments of this turbulent time in the Territory.

Charles served as governor of Kansas, beginning his only term upon the state's admission to the Union in 1861. He held many public offices afterward, including state representative and senator, and regent of the University of Kansas. Sara and Charles lived at their Oak Ridge Farm near Lawrence until their deaths—Charles in 1894, and Sara in 1911. The main campus of the University of Kansas now stands on land that the Robinsons donated to the school.

Not long after their arrival in 1855, their house nearing completion, Sara wrote confidently about the virtues of pioneer life:

> *[April] 22nd [1855]*
> *The slit-work for the stairway is set, and we are anticipating the time when we can get into the second story. How our friends in the East would pity us, did they know just how we live; but I dare say there is not one in a hundred of them who enjoys the half we do. We are deprived of no comforts, that is, of anything essential to our happiness; for coming to the real root of the matter, every one will find that the externals have but little to do with a person's real enjoyment. We have fine, even spirits, and we feel that to live, to breathe in such a country is a joy, especially on a day like this.*

Under the hill where the sun shines slimmer,
Shrunk from the eager beam,
The work goes on with a fitful glimmer,
And music for a dream.
Over the groves and moistened meadows
The steady gray hawks wing,
And down below in the shifting shadows
The merry small birds sing.

In May, Sara described the scene from her window:

24th [1855]
The roads for many days have been full of wagons – white covered,
migrant wagons. We cannot look out of the windows without
seeing a number, either upon the road through the prairie east
of us, which comes in from Kansas City, where most emigrants
leave the boats and buy wagons and provisions for the journey, or,
going on the hill west, on their way to Topeka, or other settlements
above. . . .

The Topeka Tribune
March 24, 1859
Emigration is pouring into our Territory by hundreds and
thousands. Those coming at this time will be bone and sinew of
our country. They do not come now, as in 1857, when the spirit
of speculation was up to the highest pitch, but for the purpose
of finding homes on our productive soil. We welcome them with
warm hearts and affectionate feelings.

The Natural World

In 1855, Henry S. Clubb of New York founded the Vegetarian Kansas Emigration Company with the intent of establishing a settlement where an ideal vegetarian lifestyle could be pursued. Only non-slave-owners of strong moral character who paid into the company could join the hoped-for colony. By January 1856, a site on the Neosho River, thirty miles west of Fort Scott, had been selected. At about the same time, Mr. Clubb founded the Octagon Settlement Company, similar to the Vegetarian Company in its plan for an octagonal-shaped community. The design called for the settlements to be side by side, each four miles square, divided into sixteen farms around a central park or pasture. It was hoped that this would provide the feeling of a village, helping the settlers stave off the inevitable feelings of loneliness.

Miriam Colt and her husband William joined the company, and with their two children, Miriam's parents, and her sister, Lydia, traveled with the group from New York State to the settlement along the Neosho River. Upon arrival, the group found that the houses promised by the Company's organizers had not yet been built. The one hundred weary new arrivals spent their first nights in tents pitched on the banks of the rain-swollen Neosho. The gristmill and farm tools, also promised by company leaders, never materialized. Disease, carried by the overwhelming number of mosquitoes at the river site, killed many of those who stayed. The Vegetarian Company did not survive as an organization, as many settlers became disillusioned and left the Territory. Miriam and her family remained.

Miriam's diary reflects upon not only moments in the working part of her day, but also her encounters with the natural side of what she called "that Fairy Land." She did not hide her diary away in a safe place to be pulled out at day's end, but tucked it in her apron pocket where, when time permitted, she recorded six months of her life in Kansas. In 1862, Miriam published her observations as a book, *Went to Kansas*.

May 28, 1856
Elm Creek, Kansas Territory
The spider-wort blooms in acres of blue,
around; and the sensitive plant, with its
slightly briery running stalk, covered all
over with flowers of pink balls dotted with
yellow, and its tiny leaves that shrink from the
least touch, sends out its scent of otto of roses to
meet your olfactories, some rods before you reach it.

May 30, 1856
Elm Creek, Kansas Territory
Have been over to see Mrs. H., she is some better.
Picked another bouquet of very rich flowers on
my way, and placed them for her to look at; there
were Japan lilies, large beautiful snakes-head,
larkspurs of many colors and much larger than
those we cultivated at home; prairie roses of every

shade and variegation, golden coreopsis, sweet William, and a
variety of others that were strangers to me.

In the spring of 1855, Sarah Maria Colegrove Everett left Oneida County, New York, with her husband, John, and their two young sons. They originally planned a move to Minnesota, but due to their sincere dedication to the antislavery cause, changed their destination to Kansas. On the journey their youngest son, Henry, aged six months, became ill and died. Sarah, John, and two-and-a-half-year-old Frank traveled on with saddened hearts. The family's misfortune continued. Upon arriving at their purchased claim near Osawatomie, they found it taken over by another settler and bare of the house they had contracted to build. Through similar fraudulent circumstances, not uncommon in the new territory, they lost their second claim as well. Finally, John, Sarah, and little Frank made their home, as John described in a letter to his sister, "in a very pretty little spot about 1¼ miles from the Potawatomie Creek." They named their claim Longwood Place.

Many of Sarah's letters describe sickness and struggle, especially during the winter. But as spring brought new life to the prairie, Sarah wrote joyfully of the natural beauty around her. In a letter to her sister, Jennie, in March 1859, Sarah's words are filled with the welcome relief of spring's arrival.

In a letter to another sister, she inquired about the number and variety of flowers her sister had gathered on the family farm. She continued on to paint a wonderful verbal landscape of the prairie in bloom:

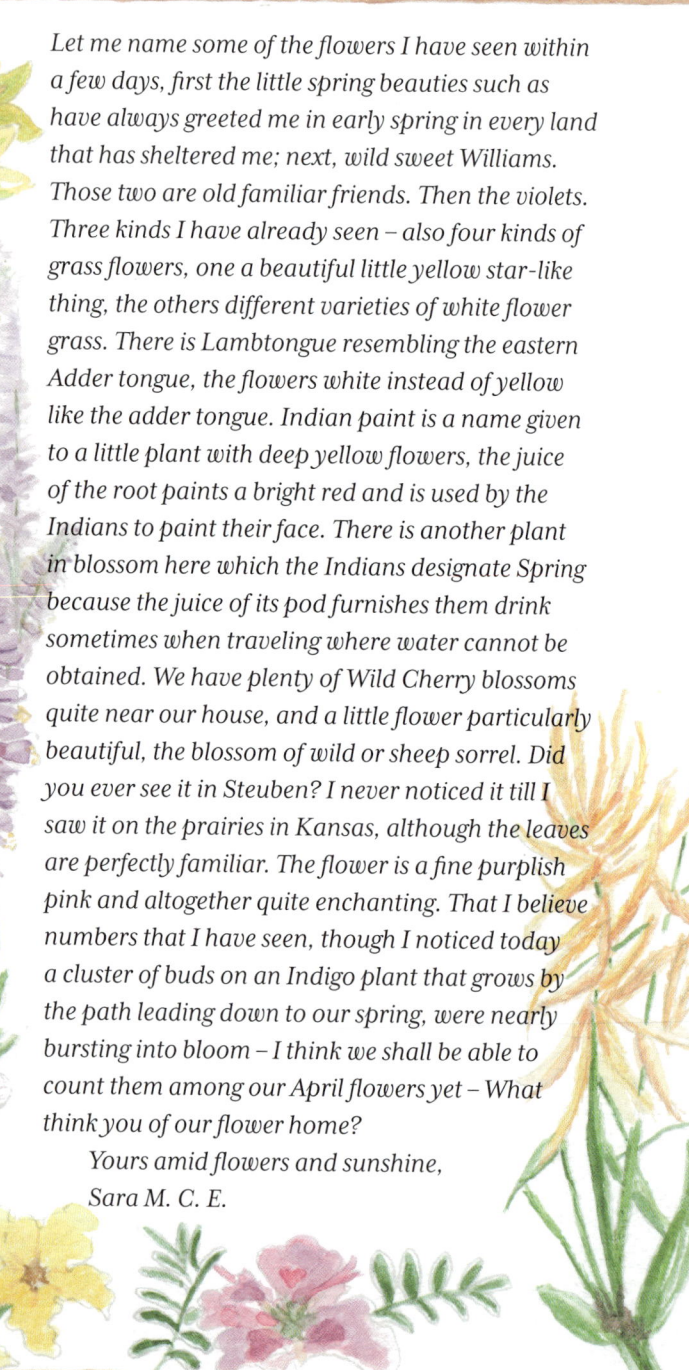

Let me name some of the flowers I have seen within a few days, first the little spring beauties such as have always greeted me in early spring in every land that has sheltered me; next, wild sweet Williams. Those two are old familiar friends. Then the violets. Three kinds I have already seen – also four kinds of grass flowers, one a beautiful little yellow star-like thing, the others different varieties of white flower grass. There is Lambtongue resembling the eastern Adder tongue, the flowers white instead of yellow like the adder tongue. Indian paint is a name given to a little plant with deep yellow flowers, the juice of the root paints a bright red and is used by the Indians to paint their face. There is another plant in blossom here which the Indians designate Spring because the juice of its pod furnishes them drink sometimes when traveling where water cannot be obtained. We have plenty of Wild Cherry blossoms quite near our house, and a little flower particularly beautiful, the blossom of wild or sheep sorrel. Did you ever see it in Steuben? I never noticed it till I saw it on the prairies in Kansas, although the leaves are perfectly familiar. The flower is a fine purplish pink and altogether quite enchanting. That I believe numbers that I have seen, though I noticed today a cluster of buds on an Indigo plant that grows by the path leading down to our spring, were nearly bursting into bloom – I think we shall be able to count them among our April flowers yet – What think you of our flower home?

Yours amid flowers and sunshine,
Sara M. C. E.

Conversations about moving west filled the streets of Philadelphia in 1856. Residents Charles and Mary Sears answered the call of adventure, encouraged by a friend who would accompany them. Charles's failing health also dictated that they leave city life behind. The couple and their eighteen-month-old daughter traveled by train and prairie schooner, finally settling in Iowa. Two and a half years later, the Sears family decided to head farther west to California, and set off once again, having promised to visit a friend in Kansas on the way. That visit lasted for twenty-five years.

Mr. and Mrs. Sears and their children, Emma and William, reached Lecompton, Kansas Territory, on the evening of July 4, 1859. Tired and weary from four weeks on the trail, the family decided to settle on a farm twelve miles southeast of Lawrence. Drought forced many to leave the Territory that summer, but the Sears family stayed on, moving into Lawrence and then to nearby Hesper, where Charles taught school in a log cabin. Recalling their return to the farm in the spring of 1860, Mary Sears wrote:

When spring came it brought rain, and we moved back to the farm. It has been said that "every bitter has its sweet." The expanding prairies were dry, but they were like a garden of flowers - beautiful pink phlox, the pink and white wild peas, the beautiful wild rose and the dainty sensitive plants, which closed at the gentlest touch; these the little ones delighted to gather and they brought them to me in lovely bouquets.

The New England Emigrant Aid Company motivated many New Englanders to organize a group for the trip to Kansas. Charles Lines of New Haven, Connecticut, heard the Company's founders give speeches in the area and commenced finding prospective members for the new Connecticut Kansas Colony that he would lead to the Territory in the spring of 1856. Lines and his group founded the town of Wabaunsee, fifteen miles east of Manhattan.

Lines spent forty-three years in Kansas, holding various public positions, including territorial legislator and regent of the University of Kansas, from 1864 to 1874. An avid horticulturist, he also founded the Kansas Horticultural Society. Documenting the progress of the Colony for the New Haven (Connecticut) *Daily Palladium,* he described the vegetation he found:

Mission Creek, K. T., April 22, '56

In traversing the prairies yesterday, for the purpose of appraising the claims taken by the members of our company, we discovered a variety of beautiful flowers, and among them the "sweet pea" in full bloom, much more beautiful than we have them in our flower gardens at the East, and of a delightful spicy odor. It would have given us very great pleasure could we have sent to our friends at home a boquet, by telegraph, made up of these various native products of "Kansas." We also noticed strawberries in full bloom, raspberries leaved out and budded, grapes in leaf, and wild hops in great profusion. We are every day more impressed with the great agricultural resources of this country, and when it becomes subdued and under genial cultivation, and the arts and privileges of a Christian civilization are established here, we can see no reason why it may not be a delightsome land, filled with abundance and variety for the sustenance and happiness of man.

The *Kansas Tribune* made its first appearance in January 1855 in Lawrence. In November 1855, John Speer moved the newspaper operation to Topeka.

The Topeka Tribune
April 6, 1857

Plant Trees

Let our Topeka friends bear in mind that now is the time to plant trees. If they would beautify the town, add to its healthiness, give it a thrifty prosperous appearance, and make a pleasant and attractive place, to strangers as well as themselves, there is no way in which they can accomplish all these objects so effectually, as by a tasty and liberal provision of fruit and shade trees along our public walks and grounds. Our forests abound with almost every variety desirable for transplanting, and the delicious coolness which they impart during the heat and glare of the summer, to say nothing of the enhanced value of property resulting from them, ought to be sufficient inducement for their cultivation.

Free-state supporter Joseph Trego journeyed to Kansas Territory three times, the first being in March 1858. On his third trip in 1858, he brought his wife and three daughters to their new home in Sugar Mound (now Mound City). Joseph operated a saw-mill on Little Sugar Creek with brothers Thomas and Edwin Smith. He had a keen interest in trees and often made notes about them in his diary.

March 1859 10 Th. warm, windy.
Procured a lot of trees; Sugar tree, Box elder, Mulberry, Horse-chestnut here – tree And Wild plum, and set them out in yard. Purpose getting some more plum trees and Mulberry to-morrow and drawing a load of hay if the wind don't continue to blow . . .

Born in 1825 in Lewis County, New York, Charles

Puffer lived in Wisconsin before eventually moving to Kansas in 1857. He and his wife Hannah settled in Burlington, seventy-five miles southeast of Lawrence, where Charles also spent time. The couple had six children. During the Civil War, Charles served as captain of Company K, Sixteenth Kansas Cavalry Regiment. After the war, he served for several years as a commissioner of public instruction on the Burlington city council. Charles also owned a lumber business and drugstore. He died on Christmas Day, 1896, and is buried in Graceland Cemetery in Burlington. In his diary, Charles described some spring scenes:

Lawrence, Kansas Territory
March 20, [1858]
Cloudy in Morning. Pleasant in after Noon. [Tending] store.
Weather warm grass springing up and Looks Green. People
preparing to make gardens.

April 4, [1858]
Cool and pleasant all went on to Mt Oriad Saw straw and
gooseberry in Blossom.

Mouth of the Big Blue River, K. T.
May 22nd, 1855

MR. EDITOR:
Game is very plenty about the Blue. Wild geese, turkeys, ducks,
prairie hens, and deer; but they don't always stop long enough for

*a ball to hit them. The rivers are full of fish of the finest flavor I ever
tasted, similar to the Eastern trout, but a richer treat for the table.
They are called catfish, and some of them weigh over 50 lbs., and
sometimes twice that amount, and the flesh when dressed, looks as
large as a fat calf. A man just above us, on the Blue River, one night
last week with a "seine" caught 1,500 lbs. and carried them the next
day to Fort Riley to market.*

    Julia Louisa Lovejoy

Education

With new communities came the need for schools. By the end
of 1859, the report issued by the Territorial Superintendent of
Common Schools revealed that school was being taught in a total of
136 schools, in fifteen counties. Several prominent citizens thought
the Territory needed an institution of higher learning. Two of those
people, Isaac T. Goodnow and his brother-in-law, Reverend Joseph
Denison, led the effort to establish a college in Manhattan.

As a young man, Isaac Goodnow studied at night and worked
during the day to support his family. He graduated and became
a professor of English and natural sciences. In 1855, he heard
a passionate antislavery speech by Eli Thayer in Providence,
Rhode Island, and soon after left for Kansas Territory with his
wife, Ellen. His motivations included not only helping in the
antislavery cause, but, as he wrote to a friend, it would also be
a good way to gain wealth and settle his wife in a more health-
ful climate.

Goodnow, like others in Kansas, viewed education as a cornerstone of building a better life for their children in years to come, and worked with his brother-in-law, Reverend Joseph Denison, to establish the college in Manhattan. Both men traveled extensively, seeking financial support for the school, which many, including the Methodist Episcopal Church, provided. In 1859, Bluemont College became a reality, opening its doors to students. Charles Julius Lovejoy enrolled, along with fifty-two others. Charles Julius had come to Kansas with his parents, Charles and Julia, and become one of Manhattan's first citizens. In 1863, the college—then known as the Kansas College of Agriculture and Applied Science—became the first school in the state land grant college system. Now Kansas State University, the school's main campus encompasses 664 acres.

Isaac and his wife Ellen built a house within sight of the Manhattan campus in 1861, and lived there until they died, in 1894 and 1900, respectively. Listed on the National Register of Historic Places, their stone house is administered by the Kansas Historical Society.

In 1858, Goodnow, in his role as agent for the college, wrote to friend Eli Thayer to solicit funding and support for the institution:

Manhattan, K. T.
May 24th, 1858
Hon Eli Thayer

My Dear Friend,
I called to see you while East last Summer but missed you. I
regretted this much as I wished a long talk on the interests of
Kansas, & especially as connected with Bluemont Central College,
an Institution already Chartered for this place. Its most striking
feature will be our Agricultural Department of a most thorough
practical character. Further particulars you can learn from Mr.
Parrott, our Delegate to [xxx] [xxx] sent statistics & a petition to
Congress for a grant of 100,000 acres of land to carry out our

*Agricultural Department Can you not bring influences to bear on
this question that will make it succeed? . . .*
  Yours gratefully & Affectionately,
  Isaac T. Goodnow

Reverend Joseph Denison emigrated to Kansas with wife,
Sarah, and their three children with the first spring party of the
New England Emigrant Aid Company in March 1855. The family
settled in Manhattan when the town was just being laid out. One
of the first trustees of the college, Denison went on to become
the school's first president. In 1860, during a time of severe
drought, Reverend Denison worked to secure donations for the
citizens of Kansas.

While he traveled to obtain funding, Denison's nephew, Henry, kept him informed on the college construction and, in this letter, described the cornerstone ceremony:

Manhattan, K. T.
May 11th, 1859

My Dear Uncle
Father received your letter dated May 7 last night. I was very glad
to hear from you. I have thought of you every day and hoped
you were having good success. Yesterday the Corner Stone of
the College was laid. They had speeches from Rev Mr Preston Mr
Blood Gen Pomeroy . . .
      From Your Affectionate Nephew
      Henry L. Denison

Thomas Wells also attended the Bluemont ceremony. Thomas had reluctantly left his family in Rhode Island for the far-off Kansas Territory in 1855. He abandoned a plan to join his father's bank after attending the academy of East Greenwich, and instead set out for the West in hopes of improving his health. His health did improve, and in a letter to his parents a few months later, Wells wrote that everyone thought he looked much healthier than when he arrived. "Indeed," he told them, "I know that I am better, not sick at all now."

Wells staked his first claim in Juniata. In May 1856 he moved to Manhattan, where he became a charter member of the Congregational Church and an integral part of the community. He married Eleanor (Ella) Bemis on October 30, 1856.

Clearly, Thomas missed his family, and each letter home contained a plea for them to come visit, or an enticing plan for them to move to Kansas. Sadly, neither event ever occurred. Thomas lived in Manhattan until his death on January 9, 1907.

In a letter to his father, he described the new college.

Manhattan, K. T.
May 14, 1859

My dear father,
. . . They had speeches &c at the laying of the corner stone of the
"Blue Mont Central College" last Tuesday afternoon, the first
ceremony of the kind that has occurred in Kansas. About three
hundred people were present and some very good speeches were
made. Quite a number of documents were placed in the cavity of
the stone. The underpinning corners, and window and door caps
to be hewn, the rest rough work. It will be in full view from our
house, half a mile distant. . . .

Love to Mother and Herbert. Hoping to hear from home soon
again I am yours affectionately

T. C. Wells

The Sabbath

On the plains of Kanzas, 70 miles west of Kanzas City
April [20], '56

MESSRS. EDS . . . We spent our Sabbath very pleasantly, having
religious service in the forenoon in the cabin of Mr. Shields, where
we took our meals, and upon slabs fitted up for the purpose,
outside and adjoining. In the afternoon we held a prayer meeting
at the same place, and such meetings we have not often enjoyed at
home. The settlers from a few adjoining cabins came in, and it was
truly affecting to witness the gratitude to God manifested by them,
that men of prayer had come to the Territory. . . .

Charles B. Lines

Chestina Bowker Allen and her husband, Asahel Gilbert Allen, arrived in Kansas Territory in 1854 from Roxbury, Massachusetts. They traveled with the third New England Emigrant Aid Company. The two settled near Rock Creek in Pottawatomie County with their five children, William, Charles, Henrietta, John, and Abbie. Chestina wrote about many aspects of Territorial life ("This morning was called to be with Mrs. Childs, a bouncing daughter made her debut into this world to breath for herself") and death ("Heard of the death of Mrs. Carrol of Wildcat, the only woman who visited me in my lone two months residence and sickness. This dear woman walked three miles to comfort me in my affliction"). Her detailed journal gives a picture of day-to-day life, including the Sabbath:

[March] 20th [1855] Let me never forget to trust and serve my Heavenly Father.

[March] 25th [1855] Rev. C. Lovejoy preached to us to day. His text was "Lovest thou me?" a truly good discourse. May it prove seed sown in good soil.

May 27th [1855] Our family attend meeting at Esq Dyer's. Preaching by Rev. Chas. Blood. A Sab. School was organized. Six classes, three male and three female teachers. Rev. Lovejoy, Mr. Nealy and Mr. Allen, Mrs Lovejoy Mrs Child and Mrs Allen: Librarian, Dr Whitehorn. The scholars were Lydia, Martha, Sarah and Mary Dyer; Wm. Chas. Jno. Henrietta and Abbie Allen; Harriet and Mary Lyman, Mary and Eudora Merris, Juliet Lovejoy, John Duncan, Abraham, Enoch and James Dyer, John Dyer, Hays, Smith, Blood, Browning, Whitehorn, Wells, Perry, Weldon, Mrs. J. Dyer, Rev Mr and Mrs Trafton and Mrs Denison.

June 3rd [1856] This pleasant Sabbath, the northern Methodist held their first meeting at the new log house of Esq Dyer. Ministers present.

Presiding Elder Good, El Lovejoy who is to have charge of the circuit embracing this place; also Trafton Denison, Griffin and Blood. A full house, increasing S. S. and good preaching were characteristic of the day. 18 individuals dined at our house on baked beans, plum pudding, bread & butter.

The Sabbath held much importance for the pioneers as a time to gather strength and encouragement from their faith and from each other, as evidenced in their writings. A Lawrence newspaper featured an article on a new church bell, the sound of which, in a new community far from home, brought comfort to all who heard it.

April 12, 1855
Lawrence, K. T.

Dear wife, it is the holy Sabbath day and a fine day it is, too . . . I
have been reading the Bible you gave me and Gilson and I have
been singing.
    Frank Mayo to his wife, Thankful

May 13th [1855]
Lawrence, K. T.

I attended a Sabbath school to-day, four miles out on the
California road. There were quite a number of children present,
with some older persons. Some little English girls were very bright
and interesting. The family at whose house the school was held
are from Ohio. They are such good people that one feels it in their
presence, and sincerity and unselfishness are manifested in their
actions. They have long been earnest workers in the cause of
humanity – have "fed the hungry, clothed the naked," and given the
"cup of cold water" to the fainting soul.
    Sara Robinson

Sunday, May 27th [1855]
Topeka, Kansas Territory

Attended divine service at the flag hotel, the meeting being held
in sleeping apartment, the beds of which are in tiers like unto the
berths on a steam boat . . . The Rev Mr Shepard preached to day
from Phillippians 3d 13 & 14 verses, divideing his subject into 3 parts
oneness of object, oneness of mind, & oneness of purpose, the whole
tenor of the discourse being very appropriate to a new country. . . .
    Joseph Miller
    From his diary

On January 3, 1855, the free-state publication, the *Herald of Freedom* newspaper, printed its second issue, believed to be the first newspaper printed in Douglas County, Kansas Territory. Along with the news of the day, the paper also printed words of encouragement and cheer:

The Herald of Freedom
April 25, 1857

The Church Going Bell

For those of us who have "lived where bells have tolled to church" the pleasant sound seems a voice of civilization and indispensable to make Sabbath on the prairies. To such the first ringing of the fine toned bell of the Unitarian church was a glad occasion. It is hung for the present in a temporary belfry, near the church, to admit the completion of the tower. Besides its service in summoning to the Sabbath worship, it daily calls our young folks to school and gives noon-time at which all rally with cheerful zeal to the support of the important institution of dinner.

Blessings on the liberal hearted man, one of the merchant princes of Boston, to whom we are indebted for this humanizing sound. It makes us feel a whole generation of where we are without it.

Entertainment

C. W. Goodlander started west from his home in Milton, Pennsylvania, in May of 1855, following, as he described it, Horace Greeley's advice to "Go west, young man, and grow up with the country." After spending time in Indiana, Goodlander traveled to

Illinois and met up with an acquaintance, George Crawford, who invited him to Fort Scott, where he and some others had "started a good town." After returning to Pennsylvania for a time to visit his family, he kept his promise to Crawford. Carrying his carpenter's tool chest, Goodlander arrived at Fort Scott in May 1858. In 1900, he published *Memories and Recollections of the Early Days of Fort Scott,* his detailed account of his life there. He died in May 1914, and is buried at Fort Scott in Bourbon County.

Vivid descriptions of the residents, including women and their fashions (e.g., skirt hoops made from grape vines) fill the pages of Goodlander's memoir. He also wrote about the social life of Fort Scott, including lodge meetings (Masons, Sons of Malta), parties, and picnics:

April, 1860
All members of the lodge wore black dominoes, and the dance was
a big success.

   The dances were generally plain quadrilles to the tunes of
"Hell on the Wabash" and "Arkansaw Traveller," and sundry tunes
that all were familiar with.

Originally from Hornellsville, New York, Willard Orvis Hubbell worked as a tinsmith in Lawrence after arriving in Kansas Territory. When not working, he spent time attending various social activities in the community, including dances. As a member of the International Order of Odd Fellows and the Ancient Free and Accepted Masons, he frequently attended lodge meetings. Hubbell married Nancy Maria Gleason in April 1860. He is buried in Lawrence, Kansas.

   Diary entries indicate that Hubbell played a musical instrument, possibly the fiddle, on various occasions.

Wednesday March 9, 1859
This forenoon I work . . . This evening I went to a surprise party
at Sterns.

Tuesday April 19, 1859
This evening a company of young people went to Franklin and had
a supper and then had a dance Pollard & I plaid a good time

Friday April 29, 1859
To work in the shop This Evening I plaid at the Eldridge Hotel we
had a good time no Lodge tonight

John Henry Deering traveled from Bath, Maine, to the Kansas Territory in 1856, and settled in Palmyra Township, near present-day Baldwin City. In 1858 he opened a wagon shop, and in his diary mentioned work on hubs, trucks, and wheels, and also of working at Baker University, then under construction. Deering married Cornelia Gifford in 1862, and the couple had seven children. Her father, Hezekiah, also settled in the Prairie City area, and John wrote often of visiting the Gifford family.

Just before the Civil War began, Deering moved his family to Leavenworth, where he worked for the government and served six months with the Missouri State Cavalry. Later he moved back to Lawrence, where he opened a drugstore. Deering passed away in 1880 and was buried in Lawrence.

The diary documents John's daily life, including his feelings of despair ("This week has been the hardest of my life") and encouragement ("Prospects look brighter . . ."). Deering's social life included visiting friends, where singing seems to have been a popular activity, and going to parties and dances. He attended meetings of the Palmyra Lodge No. 23, Ancient Free and Accepted Masons, organized in 1856, where he was a charter member. In quieter times, he read and caught up on his diary entries.

This Sunday March 14th [1858]
One year ago yesterday I started from home and arrived in Kansas
Territory the first day of April. I like the country very much and
intend to stop here . . . Also have had many pleasant times in P. C.
singing . . . Last night walked over to P City to attend sing . . .

Saturday May 22nd [1858]
Unpleasant . . . Up to Palmyra and spent the afternoon there & at
Bodwells Eve went down to Eldridges and had a dance, and party.
Made some acquaintances. Home early in the morning.

Birthdays gave families cause for parties and celebrations. In March 1856, Chestina Bowker Allen noted her son William's special day:

March 7th [1856] Wm. Is 21 today, his friends spend the jubilant eve-
with us. Elderberry wine, candy and nuts constitute refreshments.

Edward Fitch arrived in Kansas Territory with the third party of the New England Emigrant Aid Company in October 1854. As with many who traveled with him, he acted on his belief that Kansas should enter the Union as a free state. Edward had another motive: He saw the move as an opportunity to buy land and have a farm of his own. Prior to realizing that goal, Edward worked in Lawrence as a teacher and partner in a provisions store.

In 1855, Sarah Wilmarth and her family moved from Rhode Island to Lawrence, where her father Otis later opened the area's first bookstore. Sarah and Edward became friends and married in 1857. They settled on Edward's claim just south of Lawrence, where the family grew to include three children. Edward kept his parents well informed about the family and growing community. Family and friends in Massachusetts sent supplies that Edward distributed during 1859 and 1860, a time of severe drought. In his letters, Edward also wrote of the political upheaval in the Lawrence area, a narrative that continued until a month before his death on August 21, 1863, during Quantrill's raid of Lawrence. Several years after Edward's death, his dear friend, Joseph Savage, wrote about Edward in the Lawrence *Weekly Tribune*:

> *Edward P. Fitch was killed in the Lawrence raid. He was shot in his own house and his body burned up in it. A more genuine Yankee, or a truer son of freedom, never trod Kansas soil. He was actively engaged in our early struggles, and often heard the bullets of the ruffians whizzing in the air about his head. His was a generous soul, and a cheerful spirit, and the ring of his merry good-natured laugh is still heard in the echoes of the past. Fitch and I met each other late one afternoon in October, 1854 . . .*

His love of music and his friends, Joseph Savage and George Wilmarth, led Edward to his membership in the Lawrence Cornet Band. News of the Cornet Band often appeared in Edward's letters.

"Home," near Lawrence, K. T.
May 23 1857

Dear Parents
. . . I believe this is the first time I have written to you since I was
married. Well the eventful [April] 19th has passed and I am a
Married Man!!! Wonderful, ant it?
    I suppose that George Wilmarth has not been to Hopkinton
yet unless he is there now but he will be there soon I expect and . . .
I want you to see if he can bring Ed Whittemore's brass horn, "B flat
Barritone Tube" or rather "Sax Horn". Whittemore said he would
send it to me if he had a chance . . . I want it because I now belong
to a "Brass Band". We played in front of the Morrow House last
evening and are going to town to play at a Concert this evening. I
now beat the Bass Drum but should blow a Horn if I had one. . . .
    Yours in haste,
    Edward P Fitch

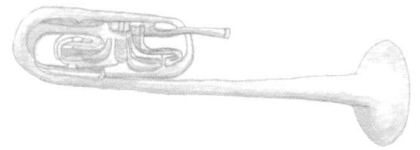

In addition to musical entertainment, both local and traveling
theatrical troupes performed in the Territory. *The Topeka Tribune*
announced and reviewed some of these dramatic offerings:

The Topeka Tribune
March 27, 1858
The Drama – We understand that next Friday evening has been fixed
upon for the first performance of the Topeka Dramatic Association,
at Museum Hall. The Association is exclusively a home production,
which fact entitles it to, as it will doubtless receive, a liberal patronage
from the people of Topeka and vicinity, especially as the corps of

performers embraces a more than ordinary degree of native dramatic talent. The Hall is a fine one, just finished, and fitted up with especial reference to the convenience of dramatic representations.

The play selected for the evening named, is entitled "The Drunkard," and is a startling exhibition of the depth and hideousness of human depravity, when ruled by the influence of the intoxicating draught.

We hope a full attendance will greet the production of this master-piece among us, and the moral which it conveys will not be lost.

The Topeka Tribune
May 29, 1858
The New England Bards will give a concert in this place in a few days. They have added an orchestra accompaniment and various other attractions to their company which enables them to promise a fine entertainment.

The Topeka Tribune
May 29, 1858
The Topeka dramatic company will give another of their elegant, chaste, and refined entertainments at Museum Hall, on Monday evening next. Those who are fond of amusement and recreation of a higher order must not fail to be on hand. The plays advertised are "Dead Shot, Secret or a Hole in the Wall," and "Kiss in the Dark."

In 1886, Frye W. Giles, one of the founders of Topeka, published his memories of life in Kansas Territory, *Thirty Years in Topeka: A Historical Sketch.* In the preface, he gave the reason for the book as "a desire that the early history of the city of Topeka might be preserved in perfect truthfulness." In addition to serving as treasurer of the founding Topeka Association, Giles served as postmaster, beginning in 1855. In his recollections, he detailed many aspects of the community, from the first building—a small log cabin—to the wide range of social events. He attended one of the Topeka performances and wrote about the play:

> The play was "The Drunkard;" the place Museum Hall, in the Ritchie block, southeast corner of Kansas and Sixth avenues. The acting was very creditable generally, and that of Dr. Charles King, in the leading part, was quite a surprise.

Early settlers of Kansas brought many experiences with them from their homes in Massachusetts, Illinois, and even England. No matter their diverse backgrounds, they all seemed to enjoy a picnic.

The Topeka Tribune
May 12, 1859
MAY PARTY. – The young folks of our city got together on Monday morning and took a stroll in the forest along the river. Bright, beautiful, and pleasant, they seemed to enjoy themselves and the occasion. They were dressed in white, their brows decked with sweet scented flowers. A few baskets of good things were prepared for the occasion and partaken of in the wood.

Topeka, May 18, 1855.
Editor, Herald of Freedom
Being appointed as a reporting committee to furnish you the proceedings of the Picnic Party, which took place in Topeka on the 17th inst., [abbreviation for the Latin "instante mensa," meaning date of the current month] and cause the same to be presented to you for publication, we, therefore, comply with this appointment, and beg leave to lay before you the following report:

Some 10 days ago the ladies of Topeka conceived the idea of getting up a picnic party, that the people of this region, who had come from different portions of our country, might have an opportunity of becoming more thoroughly acquainted with each other, and to perpetuate a custom, which is very prevalent in the East. The ball was thus set in motion, which was to bring about the happy result, which we are about to detail, and the time appointed was the 17th inst.

The morning dawned upon us, and was just cloudy enough to make it comfortable, and shield us from the scorching rays of old Sol. The copious showers of rain, which fell the night previous, effectually prevented us from being discommoded by dust. The underbrush was removed from the beautiful grove which skirts the Kansas River, by the enterprising young men of the place, and when finished, was a most lovely site for our gathering. The overhanging boughs, which nature had covered in rich green foliage, and the soft verdant carpet spread beneath our feet, made the place and the occasion delightful. In good time the ladies, of whom there was a goodly number, began to assemble, accompanied by those made of coarser material.

The table – fifty feet long – which was spread with rich viands, fairly groaned beneath its load of dainty food. There was the mammoth fish, which but the night previous was enjoying his native freedom in the murky waters of the Kansas River, now stretched at length on a large platter, prepared to grace the festive board.

A barbecue, and other like substantial food, came in for their share of attention. A large and beautiful pyramid cake, surrounded by other minor ones, graced the table, while from the apex, as if a natural product a rich profusion of prairie flowers shot forth their smiling petals . . .

One of the many toasts proposed that day:

"To the future of Topeka – May it be as full of prosperity and fruition as the present is of promise and hope."

F. W. Giles attended the picnic and remembered the day's events:

The settlers, appreciating the importance of social influences, promptly took measures to bring the persons and families to an acquaintance with each other. As there was no house reasonably spacious for one family even, it was determined to have a picnic, after their Eastern customs. The grounds between First avenue and the river were at that time covered with quite a dense growth of timber and shrubs, and yielding shade about as complete as any roof in the settlement could do; so there, on grounds now traversed by Kansas avenue, the picnic was to be held . . . The 17th of May was the day appointed for this first of all Topeka's social gatherings . . . Mrs. Ward contributed a roasted pig, of ample size, for the head of the table, and the friendly Kaw contributed a twenty-pound catfish for the opposite end.

Never did a little community of strangers work with more hearty good feeling to solace each other with sympathetic words and kindly acts. In many instances they had never met till they met on that festive occasion, and yet they appeared toward each other more like tried acquaintances and friends. The occasion was a joyful one to all participants, and left the influence of love and good will to work upon them for many years . . .

Personal Pursuits

Though working hard to establish a new way of life, settlers did find time to catch up on their individual interests. For John Deering and James Stewart, this free time meant a chance to play music and read.

Sunday 30 [April, 1858]
Prairie City, K. T.

Very pleasant weather Up to Palmyra in forenoon Down to Brooke
read Dickens, took a late dinner, and walked over to P City. Sang
at the house of Mr. Gifford. Evening, quite cool. Wrote diary for
Thursday, Friday & Sat.
John Deering

At age twenty-five, James Stewart and his brother William headed for Kansas as part of the Western Pennsylvania Company. The group shared a cause that was common among other emigrant groups of the time: to populate the Kansas Territory with people of antislavery sentiment.

By the time the Company arrived in Kansas City in November 1854, many members of the group had become disheartened, realizing that the group's affairs had been poorly managed. Cold, rainy weather and the lack of accommodations further dismayed the new arrivals. The band of two hundred settlers dispersed across the land, with some heading for Lawrence and Topeka. Others turned back for Pennsylvania.

James and William settled in Council City, Osage County. In his diary, Stewart gives a detailed account of his life in the Territory, writing about working his claim, reading, and playing his fiddle. He also recorded his thoughts about his many roles in the community, including justice of the peace, county attorney, and state legislator.

During a visit to Pennsylvania in 1862, James married Mary Newell. He and Mary lived in Council City (which became Burlingame in 1857) until 1868, when, in poor health, he returned to Pennsylvania where he died soon thereafter.

In his diary from 1855, Stewart referred to the books he was reading at the time, including *Great Harmonia*, *Young Man's Counselor*, and *American Manual*.

THUR, [April] 19 [1855]
Council City, K. T.

Cool & windy all day but moderate in the evening. Read Great Harmonia during the forenoon, went down to Hoovers in afternoon, then to Titus', thence to Freels, back to Hoovers, bought 21 lbs bacon from him, and then home, got back about 2oC[l]ock and read Great Harmonia balance the day.
    THUR., [April] 26.
    Cool north wind but not unpleasant. Worked in the garden & read alternately all day.
    TUES., [May] 1.
    Cloudy, a light shower about noon, and a little rain through the day. Worked all day in the garden, finished reading Great Harmonia in the evening.
    WED., [May] 2.
    Cloudy & a few drops of rain in the forenoon, clear & pleasant in the afternoon. Worked in garden as usual and forenoon, went down town to attend settlers meeting in afternoon . . .writing a constitution for a literary society, worked at it for some time and then commenced reading Young Man's Counselor, read some time and retired to bed. The settlers meeting was of no account, had no object in view & did nothing. Brother and I seperated to day, he removing to his own cabin. After the settlers meeting adjourned, a few of us holding an informal meeting to consult about organizing a literary society, we appointed a committee to make a constitution, myself chairman.
    SUN., [May] 27.
    Pleasant all day. Read in the American Manual some time, took a good bathe, eat dinner, & went down town. Loafed round sometime. Came home, had Young onions and radishes for supper, finished reading American Manual and commenced Olneys family book of history, read a few Chapters in the bible.

Homesickness set in quickly for many settlers. Letters from home with the latest news helped to fill the void. Family and friends in the East anxiously awaited word from Kansas. Joseph Miller, who camped near the future site of Topeka, traveled to Lawrence and, after leaving the meetinghouse, asked about letters at the post office there:

Tuesday, April 24th 1855
Topeka, Kansas Territory

As soon as I made my exit I hasted to the post office to enquire for letters, the gentleman who had charge of the office had not risen, but on my rapping at the door, he soon made his appearance and on my interogateing as to my errant he retired within & soon handed me a letter from my dear wife, the first I had received since leaving home. Oh! It was like cold watter to a thirsty soul, & the shadow of a great rock in a weary land. I devoured its contents with eager avidity, for it was like a feast of fat things, with wine on the lees, it told me of the dear ones I had left behind, and that they were all well.

    Joseph Miller
    From his diary

Oscar Leonard arrived in Lawrence, Kansas, in the autumn of 1855. He relocated in the spring of 1857, helping to found the city of Burlington in Coffey County. In an April 6, 1856, letter to his family, he updated them on his situation, described the growing town of Lawrence, and requested more frequent letters:

April 6th 1856
Lawrence, Kansas Territory

My Dear Parents and Sister,
Once again I sieze my pen to communicate with you from this my
distant and strangely romantic retreat . . .
For the present I am staying with an old friend of mine here
formerly from Vermont. We are farming a little as he has a farm
near town. I enjoy myself well and can hardly realize that I am so
far away from my New England home, as most of the inhabitants
are from Yankee land which gives a familiar air to things,
unknown in most western towns.
Of my future intentions and the country I will write you
hereafter. Lawrence a town of no small notoriety with you I
presume, has one of the most delightful sites I have ever seen, at
present numbering about one thousand souls and souls that are
true and tried. The town is fortified at each entrance with the Stars
and Stripes still floating on the wind. Presents quite a formidable
appearance. It is growing rapidly and will become a town of
importance–more anon–I wish you would adopt the plan of
writing me every week so that despite mail delay I may hear from
you occasionally at least.
My health is excellent, the weather fine and farmers busily
at work. Ever mindful of you all and hopeful of your health and
happiness I am
Yours
O.E.L.

Thoughts on Kansas
Kansas Tribune, May 23, 1855
Hope

O'er life's moving waters, our bark swiftly gliding,
Hope's visions, like sunbeams, fall bright and serene –
They pour their warm glow through our bosoms confiding;
Nor dream we, that shadows shall darken the scene;
Thus down the smooth current of life sweetly flowing,
Warm hearted and blissful we'll skim o'er the tide –
Each object divine, in the mellow light glowing,
With rapture we'll hail, as enchanted we glide.

What, though from our view each bright prospect be clouded,
And Time steal away the sweet blossoms he gave,
And hopes that once cheered us, in darkness are shrouded,
Or buried, like diamonds, beneath a dark wave –
Yet Hope, for a clime of more permanent pleasure,
Beams bright through each storm that o'er shadows our way,
Where loved ones, and lost, are restored, and each treasure
Unfading shall bloom in perfection of day.

Summer

My husband and self have been spending some
of the hours of this Sabbath-day in writing to
our good friends away in the northern land.
We have given them a description of this "fairy
land" though we would not trouble them with
any disclosures of disappointments, etc.; for we
mean to live above and outgrow them, make
us a home in this sunny south, garlanded with
vines, embossed around with many flowers,
and wearing the halo of true and loving hearts.

Miriam Colt
June 12, 1856

Overland emigration to Kansas slowed during summer months
due to hot, dry conditions. However, trains still left New England,
and Missouri River steamboats docked in Kansas City with
the Territory's newest citizens. Journalists, including William
Tomlinson, continued to publish articles and guidebooks for travel
to, and settlement in, Kansas.

As Miriam Colt suggested in her diary entry from June of 1856,
disappointment did play a role in Territorial life. Settlers who had
the resolve and resources to persevere through the adversities they

encountered, stayed. Many who possessed neither returned to the comfort and familiarity they had known before coming to Kansas. Some individuals arrived in the Territory with no plans, money, or supplies, expecting somehow to find everything they wanted or needed waiting for them, only to turn back after one or two days, sadly disappointed. Many settlers came as prepared as they thought possible, but later met with illness or the loss of a loved one. Reverend James Griffing and Joseph Savage belonged to the latter group, both having to deal with sickness and personal loss. Despite their hardship, they remained devoted to the life and people they had become acquainted with in the Territory, contributing greatly to its character and history.

Although emigration continued, it slowed in 1856 due to violence—sometimes deadly—between opposing political groups on the issue of the Territory's status. The year 1856 became a year of exodus from the struggling communities. For those who remained, Mother Nature provided little consolation, as a lack of rain choked the crops that had been planted by hopeful newcomers. The situation, well publicized in the East, resulted in the arrival of supplies from both individuals and aid organizations, including churches. On August 10, 1857, the *Herald of Freedom* ran an item announcing "Clothing for Kansas," to be distributed at the Unitarian Church. According to the notice, "There are several hundred boxes and barrels of bedding and wearing apparel." Also in August 1857, E. B. Whitman, an agent of the National Kansas Committee, submitted an expense sheet that showed supplies sent to settlers. Hope and survival arrived in the form of bedding, clothing, seeds, and vegetables.

After the hard work of spring tilling and planting, the early summer months found settlers waiting to see what the earth would yield. In addition to feeding themselves and their families, some hoped to sell extra produce to local merchants, including Charles Stearns. An August 1855 advertisement for Stearns's store announced that the proprietors offered all kinds of supplies for sale, offering good prices for local "Butter, Cheese, Lard, Eggs, Potatoes, Melons, &c."

John Stillman Brown and Samuel Reader both wrote to family about their gardens, and also the abundant wild fruit available. In 1857, the *Kanzas News* of Emporia reported on bumper crops, including buckwheat. But crop yields and hopes both ran low in 1860, when a nine-month drought once again left the Kansas earth parched and settlers hungry. Many, disappointed and defeated, left the Territory. Struggling to survive, many of those who stayed once again received help from neighbors, churches, and aid organizations.

Summer brought hot weather. Whether working, sitting, or traveling, settlers dealt with the heat that covered the Territory from Manhattan to Osawatomie, where on July 9, 1856, as Jane Carruth wrote to her cousin, Melinda, "The thermometer stands, at eleven, at 104 in the shade . . ." Not complaining, she continued, ". . . but I like it . . . The country and climate are very delightful. . . ."

Returning to Lawrence in August 1855, Edward Fitch wrote to his family that "Thurs. was a hot day. Fri. was hotter & Sat/ was the hottest day I have seen. The thermometer stood at 105 in the shade . . ." Animals, not bothered by the weather, made appearances everywhere—shade and sun, indoors and out—as detailed by Sara Robinson and others. Frogs, birds, fish, and troublesome mosquitoes all made their presence known. Along with wild creatures, domestic animals such as cows and chickens made their way into the settlers' journals and correspondence. In a letter to his son, John Stillman Brown wrote, ". . . we have at present four cows – two calves take the milk of two – we have four oxen luxuriating on the prairie grass & waxing fat. . . ."

Summer activities provided many opportunities for socializing. Weddings, Fourth of July festivities, and dances all took place during the summer months. With the issues of popular sovereignty in national news, Fourth of July celebrations in the Territory took on special significance, both to those who attended and to the rest of the nation as well. Accounts of Independence Day events filled newspapers, journals, and letters. For quieter times, finding a shady spot to read a book, letter, or newspaper from home could be relaxing and comforting. The exchange of letters and newspapers between Kansans and family and friends chronicled events, filled in details on each other's locality, and helped to maintain important connections between old home and new.

In her recollections, Anna Margaret Randolph, who had settled in Emporia with her family in 1858, wrote about the summer of 1859:

> *As the end of summer that year of 1859 drew near, the settlers were cheerful, hopeful and happy. Border warfare was a thing of the past. We were getting the upper hand of the ague that had so drained and crippled our energies. We had made our homes a little more comfortable. . . .*

Emigration

The Kanzas News (Emporia and Linn County)
August 1, 1857

Scarce a day passes but long trains of wagons, filled with the "wife and little ones" and furniture of the hardy pioneer pass through

*this place. Many of them push on towards the Verdigris, or still
farther on to the Walnut and Little Neosho, while numbers go up
or down the Neosho and Cottonwood, "setting their stakes" on
some of the many vacant claims along those streams.*

*Next fall will witness such a "covered wagon" emigration into
Kanzas as was never before seen.*

In the spring and summer of 1858, William Tomlinson, a correspondent for the *New York Tribune,* traveled throughout Kansas Territory. He compiled his notes into a book, *Kansas in Eighteen Fifty-Eight,* published in 1859. In the preface, Tomlinson explained his objectives in writing the book were first, to correct what he felt was misinformation on the state of affairs in Kansas, and on what he called the "difficulties" in the Territory. *Difficulties* referred to incidents related to the pro-slavery/antislavery controversy. He felt a "duty," as he described it, to the free-state settlers to present a true and unbiased picture. Secondly, he wanted to make a record of the events for future historians.

In the book, Tomlinson related his observations regarding the settling of the Territory:

*Emigration continued to flow rapidly into the Southern part of
the Territory, and the most desirable claims near and along the
timbered streams of the country, were rapidly taken up by the
new comers. Many of these emigrants were young men, without
families, who came to Kansas to secure homes for themselves
while plenty of good land was still remaining in the hands of
the government. Nearly all were looking forward to an early
settlement in life with that loved one, either in flesh and blood
being, or in Utopia.*

The Natural World

Along with historical and political events, William Tomlinson recorded information about the climate, soil, and geography of the area to aid future emigrants. He provided vivid descriptions of the natural environment:

The scenery is particularly pleasing. Generally speaking, throughout the West there is a sameness of landscape, but in Kansas the scenery is ever varying. Mound, valley, stream and woodland all combine to give it a charm, and it only needs the hand of art to make it one of the most substantially beautiful countries in the world. Its sky is also one of the clearest and loveliest that over-arches the earth. I do not think that Italy itself can possess a more gorgeous heaven than Kansas. Some of its cloud and sunset views are grand beyond words, and I have gazed on them at times until my whole soul has been filled with the emotions awakened by their loveliness. The natural loveliness of Kansas is remarked by almost all who visit it, who have any eye for the beauty of nature.

As an agent of the New York Kanzas League, George Walter collected and published information for prospective settlers in his guide *History of Kanzas, Also Information Regarding Routes, Laws, etc.,* published in 1855. He described the natural and political environment, and included advice on routes and necessary supplies. Information on available timber, fundamental in the growth of communities, included a list of observed species:

Forest Trees
Trees are the White and Black
Walnut, Hickory, or Shell
Bark, Oak (several varieties),
Beach, Maple, Birch, Bass,
Sassafras, Sycamore,
Butternut, Ash, Cotton Wood,
Lindon, Wild Cherry, Locust,
Elm, Red-Cedar, Mulberry,
Coffee-Bean, &c.

In 1856, James Harrison Carruth, his wife Jane, and their four children arrived in Osawatomie, Kansas Territory. After a long journey from Watertown, New York, the family initially made their home in a tent pitched on land owned by an agent of the New England Emigrant Aid Company. James believed in the free-state cause of the company. In a letter to her cousin describing their arrival, his wife, Jane, wrote, "We arrived here safe and pretty sound, considering all things, and are quite happy in our tent on the ground." James, a Presbyterian minister and science teacher, later became professor of natural sciences at Baker University and served as the state botanist from 1868 to 1892. James and Jane died in 1875 and 1897, respectively. They are buried in Oak Hill Cemetery in Lawrence.

Lucy, the Carruths' only daughter, wrote to her friend Fannie soon after getting settled in Osawatomie:

Our Tent, Osawatomie
June 1, 1856

Dear Fannie:
Here we are, safe and sound, in
the little village of Osawatomie.
One of the Mr. Grants of
Antwerp, who started with us,
is going back in a day or two,
and I thought it would be a good
chance to send a letter. . . .

I should like to have you
give me a balloon visit. What
would you think of flowers
up to your neck! Here is
spiderwort, phlox prairie pea,
wild verbena (a most beautiful

flower), scarlet milkweed, roses (as many as you could wish), and a great many others that I do not know the names of. I shall save many kinds of seeds this fall. We have a great deal of fruit on our claim – gooseberries, grapes, plums, mulberries, raspberries, and others.

We have gooseberries with every meal. . . .

Lucy Carruth

Neosho River, West of Fort Scott
Kansas Territory
June 12th [1856]

Yesterday father gave us an invitation to take a ride out into this roadless country. Soon Mrs. V, sister L., myself and children were in our covered wagon, and the oxen bore us slowly over the prairie, nipping and crushing the flowers as they went. The first of June is the time for flowers–the broad, wild parterre is now glowing with thousands of them, from the richest hue to the most delicate tint. We passed broad beds of portulacca blooming in the richness in the bright sunshine, while near its large beds of bright sunny flowers, the prickly pear was growing in luxuriant clumps, ornamented with large yellow flowers dotted with black, which on touching would give sharp intimations of their nature.

Miriam Colt
From Went to Kansas

In his guidebook, *History of Kanzas*, George Walter provided potential settlers with a list of wild fruit he observed during his travels in the state:

Wild Fruit
The country abounds with the Plum (four or five varieties), Cherry,
Paw-Paw, Persimmon, Grape (several varieties), Hickory Nut,
Black Walnut, Butter-nut, Hazel-nut, Bean-nut, Wild Cherry,
Crab Apple, Mulberry, Strawberry, Raspberry, Gooseberry,
Blackberry, &c.

Samuel James Reader arrived in Kansas Territory in May 1855 with his sister Elizabeth, his Aunt Eliza, and Eliza's husband, Joseph Cole. Samuel settled on a claim near the pro-slavery town of Indianola, Kansas Territory, although he favored a "free" Kansas. He had limited schooling, but taught himself many skills, including French and shorthand. These both appear throughout the diary, along with paintings and sketches of various events, making his record a colorful, sometimes whimsical, look at pioneer life. Samuel began keeping a journal at age thirteen and recorded each day's events until just before his death in 1914, at age seventy-eight. In 1867, Samuel journeyed back to his boyhood home of La

Harpe, Illinois, to marry Elizabeth Smith. The couple returned to Indianola and had three children, only one of whom lived to adulthood. In addition to recording local events and weather, Samuel also wrote about what he did on and around his claim, including picking berries in the summer:

> *Sat June 23 [1855]*
> *Cool. Walled all the stone that would do . . . C & I got another load of stone. PM I got another load. C. in town to see what could be done with the whiskey dealers. Got home early! E. F. and I went below Pappans and got 8 qts of raspberries. Pleasant, nice.*

> *Wednes June 27 [1855]*
> *C. went to attend the sale of lots in town. E. J. and I went and got a water pail 2/3 full of raspberries. Saw a Kaw.*

> *Thursday June 28 [1855]*
> *I went out; got a lot of berries*

Plums and a variety of berries grew in abundance in many parts of eastern Kansas Territory. Settlers often described the fruits and their fruit-picking outings in letters and diaries:

Sugar Mound, Kansas Territory
Tues., Aug. 24, 1858
Dull. Sawing logs. A party consisting of Marias Howard, Simpson, Kate & myself went for plums. We obtained about 4 bushels in all: found most of them on Big Sugar in vicinity of Paris.
> *Joseph Trego*
> *From his diary*

Juniata, Kansas T.
Aug. 9/55
Mrs. Thomas P. Wells

Dear Mother,
. . . I had an invitation to go on
a grape hunt last Monday, with
about a dozen young people of
both sexes and had a nice time. I may tell you more about it some
other time. They were the smallest grapes I ever saw, not much
larger than our whortleberries, but when ripe are quite good.
Wild plums grow about here, I have found some plum bushes
up the creek that hang very full indeed but they are not yet ripe. . . .

Yours affectionately
T. C. Wells

Juniata, Kansas T.
August 29/55
Mrs. Thomas P. Wells

My Dear Mother,
I have neglected writing to you for some time past, waiting to
receive a letter from you first, but it does not come and I will put
off writing no longer. . . .
. . . A number of [us] went plumming yesterday. I have been
once before. We had a pleasant time and came home loaded with
as many plums as we could bring.
They grow on bushes not much larger than our current
bushes, they would grow larger, but the prairie fires keep them
down. The plums were very thick and so ripe that we could
scarcely touch the bushes without shaking them to the ground.
These plums are of a yellowish red when ripe, are nearly as large

as our tame plums and are very sweet and good. I have saved
some of the seed to carry east. . . .
  Yours affectionately,
  Thomas Wells

Born in New Ipswich, New Hampshire, in 1806, John Stillman Brown attended Phillips Exeter Academy, Dartmouth College, and Union College in New York, where he graduated in 1834. He taught agriculture in Vermont and Massachusetts for several years. He married Mary Ripley in 1836. After being ordained as a Unitarian minister in 1844, Brown served as pastor to churches in New Hampshire and Massachusetts. He moved to Kansas Territory in 1857, where he farmed for several years. He also preached and lectured in the area. Brown went on to serve the community in several capacities, including pastor of the Unitarian Church in Lawrence and superintendent of public schools in Lawrence and Douglas County. He died in 1902. In letters to his son, William, who also attended Phillips Exeter Academy in New Hampshire, Brown gave vivid descriptions of the farm and garden, and his life in Kansas. He also included fatherly advice and instructions on personal conduct:

Lawrence K. T. (Sumner Terrace)
June 21, [1857]

Dear Son William
. . . It is very dry–We have had green peas-picked a mess some
weeks ago–our corn looks quite well, though it is small. I have a
few sweet potatoe plants set out. Our tomatoes are so late that I
fear we shall not have many our vines melon & squash are such
favorites with the bugs that I fear they will devour the whole–The
gooseberries are abundant–we make sauce of them in their green
state, there are hundreds of bushes of them on our claim–then we
have the fruit bearing Mulbury–Strawberries have not been plenty.

The grape vines of which I have some 80 set out this spring look well–my little peach trees are dead–we have at present four cows–two calves take the milk of two–we have four oxen luxuriating on the prairie grass & waxing fat. I must now leave my letter & get tea–may all blessings rest on you.

Be a good boy and forget no duty–Grow in favor with God and man. Give no occasion for your instructors to speak otherwise than well of you–take good care of your health. Become a man physically, as well as mentally morally–I am very well Kind regards to Mr Soule & also to Dr Leonard & family–Do you Ever call upon them. I wish you would.

Truly & affectionately Yours
John S Brown

The Kanzas News
Emporia, Linn County
June 20, 1857

The Crops

The crops in this vicinity, under the influence of the fine growing weather of the past two weeks have come up nicely, and are growing with astonishing rapidity. One of our farmer friends in this neighborhood says his corn grows so fast that he "can hear it fairly crack!" Potatoes are doing finely, and also all kinds of garden vegetables. A great many persons here are preparing to sow Buckwheat the first of next month. This is right as we shall have facilities for grinding at home.

The Kanzas News
July 4, 1857

Buckwheat

While every Kanzas farmer is striving to put in every ounce of grain possible, last, but not least, comes buckwheat, bringing up the van of the summer crops. The present season promises to be a good one for this grain, inasmuch as the late rains in this region leaves the ground more moist; and we are in hopes also that, as we had an early spring drought, the clerk of the weather may have changed the programme of the two previous seasons, so as to give us occasional rains during the summer. Buckwheat as an article of food speaks to us for itself in the remembrance of the light dun batter-cakes, whose graceful aroma, as they come fresh from the griddle, never fails to give appetite even to the most fastidious stomach. And as we expect great things from the Sorgham Cane, whose syrup has a flavor similar to the Maple syrup; we have an additional incentive to sow buckwheat. . . .

Several of the first settlers in Kansas began planting orchards shortly after their arrival in 1855 and 1856. Samuel Reynolds, one of those early farmers, gave a report on the history of horticulture in the state to the Douglas County Horticultural Society that appeared in the *Lawrence Democratic Journal* in June 1906. According to Reynolds, the soils of Douglas County provided good drainage and nutrients, suitable to fruit production. The early orchardists tried many varieties of apples, including Pippin, Vandevere, Winesap, Maiden's Blush, and others. Reynolds's report included information on Joseph Savage from Vermont, whose farm, Spring Hill, had been named by friend Edward Fitch:

The Lawrence Democratic Journal
June 22, 1906

Joseph Savage came to Kansas from Vermont in 1854, and the next year began to plant apple trees in the newly turned sod. Many of his trees came from Vermont and were of varieties popular in that state. Some of them were quite unsuitable to our soil and climate. He raised and sold, however, a great many bushels of apples. He also planted peach trees quite extensively, both budded sorts and seedlings. He was an enthusiastic horticulturist and was for many years a valuable member of this society. . . .

In addition to their gardens and crops, many diarists included a few words on the weather. The author of this article on weather, however, described a lengthy and beautiful scene that followed recent rains:

The Herald of Freedom
Lawrence, Kansas Territory
August 10, 1857

After a Shower

A most pleasant landscape is presented to the view in our broad, far stretching prairies, after the invigorating influences of a shower. Nature seems to have gathered fresh energies from the falling drops, and everywhere starts into new and more vigorous life; while the thick foliage of the woods glistens in the coming sun. Far as the eye can reach, to the south and west, but one unbroken world of green unfolds itself to the vision, and seemingly about a mile to the east

*of south Blue Mound rises even yet more darkly against the leaden
horizon. The river, too, feels the influence of the welcome shower,
and rising rapidly, it flows on with renewed power through varied
scenes to swell the tide of the rolling Missouri, and that too, in turn
contributes to the "Father of Waters."*

Above the Missouri hung the summer sky. One evening, Miriam
Colt looked up, and painted a verbal image of the scene:

*Neosho River, west of Fort Scott, K. T.
June 15, [1856]*

*Kansas moons have been described as equaling Italy's moons in
loveliness. What Italy's moons are I know not by experience, but
the moons here are lovely far beyond describing words. The "pale
Empress of night" floats up into the blue sky studded with golden
gems, with her milky drapery on, bending the zenith almost down
with her pure robes. The gentle acclivity, the slowly declining
prairie swell, the deep ravine, the white arms of the Sycamore, the
drooping willow, the dry oak the rich flowers and pearly dew, all
reflect with angel purity her soft, mellow, and fleecy light. Who can
look on scenes like these, without being bathed to the [s]pirits care
with a feeling of holy adoration and ardent prayer to God?*
    Miriam Colt
    From Went to Kansas

In and near the rivers, under the summer sky, A. J. Hoole, Sara
Robinson, and others saw and heard some of the animal residents
close by, and John Ingalls found evidence of life that existed in the
area long before any humans arrived.

Born and raised in Darlington, South Carolina, Axalla John
Hoole taught school for twelve years before moving to Kansas
Territory with his new bride, Elizabeth. The couple lived in Kansas

for two years, during which time the pro-slavery party elected him probate judge of Douglas County. He returned to South Carolina in December 1857, and later fought in two major Civil War battles, the First Battle of Manassas (1861) and the Battle of Chickamauga (1863), where he was killed. In letters home to the women of the family, Hoole gave accounts of domestic life, acquaintances, and mentioned only briefly incidents between pro-slavery and free-state settlers. He explained to his mother and sister: "I expect you will hear enough of this in the other letters which I write home to the men folks." In the summer of 1856, he described a recent fishing trip to his sister:

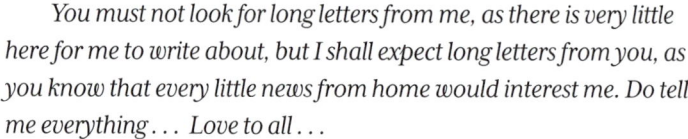

Douglas, K. T.
Sunday June the 22nd, 1856

My Dear Sister
I have seated myself to write you a few lines; I will not promise you a long letter as I don't think I can find much to write that would be interesting to you, but perhaps I may fill a sheet before I close. . . .

I went fishing yesterday and caught a fish that weighed about a pound and a half, called here a hickory shad. The man who went with me caught a pretty good catfish, both of which I took. Ate the shad this morning for breakfast, & Betsie is cooking the cat for dinner. I saw a man catch a buffalo that would weigh about 10 lbs., and another man had one to the top of the water that he thought would weigh 20 lbs. The buffalo is very much like the redhorse. . . .

You must not look for long letters from me, as there is very little here for me to write about, but I shall expect long letters from you, as you know that every little news from home would interest me. Do tell me everything . . . Love to all . . .
Your ever affectionate Brother,
A. J. H.

June 23, 1856
Neosho River, west of Fort Scott

We have been giving attention to the description of Big Creek—
but now, at the commencement of this lovely Eve, we are sitting
about our cabin door—grand-pa and grand-ma seated on the
high threshold, the rest of us on stones—Willie climbing on to
his papa's lap—Mema stands by my side—all listening to the
song of one lone whippowil, which comes up from some shady
dell by the river's side. The thousands of frogs now break in
with their melodies, from the soprano peeper, up to the bass
"grout"—and here, too, come swarms of mosquitoes about our
ears, with their "cousining" chorus, which we are trying to drive
away with smoke.

 Miriam Colt
 From Went to Kansas

June 10, 1857
Lawrence, Kansas Territory

Was awakened by a little tree-toad on my pillow this
morning. He must have climbed up
the low roof of the ell part, and in at
the window. I found a mouse in the
tub, and a swallow came into the

kitchen flapping his wings wildly, and seeming
much frightened, as we were at breakfast.

 Sara Robinson
 From Kansas: Its Interior and Exterior Life

John James Ingalls arrived in Kansas in the autumn of 1858. In initial correspondence to his father in Massachusetts, he wrote of his disappointment in what he found in "that Promised Land." In 1857, Ingalls had been admitted to the bar, having graduated from Williams College two years before. Though disheartened at first, Ingalls remained in Kansas, establishing a distinguished life of public service. He played an important part in state history, holding many political offices, including state senator and United States senator from 1873 to 1891. His interest in literature and journalism led him to help found *Kansas Magazine*. Ingalls died in Las Vegas, New Mexico, in 1900, and is buried in Atchison, Kansas. In a letter to his father in 1860, the two-year resident writes of fossils and the natural beauty around him:

Atchison, Kansas
21.8 mo 1860

Dear Father,
My memories of Appledore are very pleasant though they have
rather a limited range – being derived from a week residence there in
the Summer of 1854. The memory of the cool fresh breeze from the
waste of waters, the plunge and sway of the restless surges and the
vague sad suggestions of the mysterious sea, have often recurred to
me since I have been restricted to the monotone of the river and the

prairie. But these *Even are not without*
their charm to *the lover of nature,*
nor destitute of *the strongest interest*
to the student of *science. The theory*
of the formation *of continents by*
slow accretions *beneath incumbent*
oceans, and *their subsequent*
upheaval by some *interior force has here*

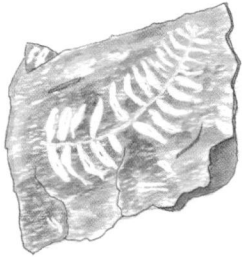

abundant confirmation. The primitive strata in broken and irregular
masses protrude through the later limestone, locked in whose stony

volume lies the history of innumerable generations of animal and vegetable existence. Fossils of the most delicate and beautiful ferns spread their tracery upon the surface of Every fractured rock: shells of Every shape and size, from whose lining membrane the pearly luster has not faded are disposed in layers as they were left by the receding billows of that unremembered sea, while Evidence of the Existence of lower but not less perfect & beautiful organisms are revealed by the microscope in Every road side stone . . .

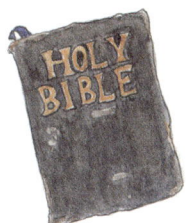

The Sabbath

Born in Whitingham, Vermont, in 1807, William Goodnow entered the printing profession as a young man. He served for a time as an apprentice and later published several newspapers in Maine. William married Harriet Paddleford in 1829. Their family grew to four, but their son and daughter both died very young. Goodnow later became a merchant and bookseller and also had a house-building business in Massachusetts.

Holding antislavery beliefs, Goodnow early on supported the New England Emigrant Aid Company cause, and traveled with a group of two hundred others, leaving Boston on March 13, 1855. Harriet chose not to join him. As one of the founders of Manhattan, William's brother Isaac had gone to Kansas the previous autumn. William joined in developing the town, opening and operating the first general merchandise store and building many of Manhattan's early structures. In keeping with his interest in newspapers, he served as a Western correspondent for papers in the East, keeping readers informed on events in the young Territory. Each week

William also corresponded with Harriet, detailing day-to-day life in his beloved new land. Apprehensive about leaving her life in Maine, and later dealing with poor health, Harriet never traveled to Kansas. Instead, William made many trips to visit her. In 1876, William died at the age of sixty-nine, and is buried in Manhattan. In one of his letters to Harriet, William told her about the local Sunday schools, and described the character of the community and its citizens:

Shannon, Wild Cat Creek, K. T.
June 10th, 1855

My Dear Wife -
. . . There has been preaching here in Isaacs cabin to-day by Rev. Mr. Trafton from Alfred, Maine – 16 persons present – there are two other meetings 3 & 6 miles from here to-day. We are well supplied with ministers in this section. The first Sab. School was organized two weeks ago 6 miles off, & another one is expected to be formed on our city cite 3 miles off another Sabbath – The most of our community are Christian enterprising persons, & we seem now from all circumstances to be a prosperous & happy people in a short time, bound to enjoy a charming climate of great natural productions & beauty & of a moral community in truth, all particulars of which I shall not now write, but some of which you may soon see announced in a new paper which is about being established in our new City of Manhattan, of which I shall probably have the charge. It is expected a full history of our first settlement & present prospects will be published & you will then, I hope, see them & judge for yourself . . .
        Yours,
        Wm. E. Goodnow

William's brother Isaac and others also chronicled Sabbath activities:

Manhattan, Kansas Territory
June 1st 1856

Sabbath. Preaching at my house P.M. by Br. Denison. Quite a large
company present. Read as usual.
  Isaac Goodnow
  From his diary

Cedar Creek, Kansas Territory
June 11 [1855]

My dear Mother,
. . . We do have meeting once a day on the Sabbath at Mr. Dyer's
also an interesting S. School both conducted by Methodists. There
are meetings held in other places in the neighborhood but too far
off for us to attend as we should have to go nine or ten miles each
way and that takes too long Sunday afternoon. . . .
  Yours affectionately,
  Thomas Wells

Council City, Kansas Territory
SUN. [July] 3, [1855]

Pleasant all day, a few drops of rain about
noon. Took a bathe in the morning dressed
up and went down to Sunday school. After
the Sunday school, I remained to hear
the Reverend Lowry preach. Came
home after sermon & wrote two letters.
Fiddled some, feel encouraged to-day.
  James Stewart
  From his diary

Miriam Colt desperately missed her home in New York. Despite her desire to leave Kansas, her father-in-law insisted the family stay. Her homesickness, combined with disappointment in the state of affairs of the fledgling Vegetarian Company, made her "sad and sorrowful" as she wrote in her diary in June 1856. The day after that entry, however, she wrote about the Sabbath and the therapeutic effect of Kansas life:

Neosho River, West of Fort Scott
June 15th [1856]

Church at Mr. Clubb's. This is a bright, lovely, quiet Sabbath day; surely, a Sabbath serenity is diffused over all. All nature is silently praising the Divine Upholder; and shall we not praise Him too? though with a saddened tone. The air is sweet and pure now, and a mild breeze is blowing from the southwest. Others have written of a vitality in the atmosphere of Kansas that is truly wonderful, "it breathes new life around, and vigor and buoyancy is felt coming back to old limbs." My health has not been so good for years, as since I have been in the Territory; my headaches have lost the greater share of their severity, and I feel equal for any task. I never was so thin in flesh, and never felt such agility.
    Miriam Colt
    From Went to Kansas

In 1856, E. S. Whitney relocated to the Territory with her husband, Thaddeus, a carpenter. Thaddeus had agreed to build a house in Lawrence for Hiram Hill, his wife's uncle. Hill owned several properties in the growing town and traveled between Lawrence and his home in Williamsburg, Massachusetts. Mrs. Whitney kept her uncle updated on his properties in Kansas and also gave accounts of local activities during his absence:

Sumner, Kansas Territory
Aug 20th [1856]

Dear Uncle Hiram,
I feel half ashamed to address you, it has been so long since you left,
& I suppose you have not had a line direct from us, since you left
. . . I am not sorry yet that I came to Kansas. If we are to become
martyrs to freedom, we never can die in a juster cause. And there
is such an opportunity of doing good here, if a person only has the
disposition.
    We have a little Sabbath school at our house at 4 o clock in
the afternoon. We usually go down town in the morning & stop at
Sabbath school in Lawrence & then are home in season for our own.
. . . Are you not coming to Kansas this summer. We should be very
happy to see you. . . .
    Please write us soon & I will engage not to be so neglectful for
the future.
    Yours Truly
    E. S. Whitney

Celebrations

In 1855, Fourth of July celebrations took place for the first time
in Kansas Territory. Newspapers announced and described the
events. As the population grew over the next few years, the number and type of Independence Day observances increased. Some
settlers joined in local festivities, while others, like Samuel Reader,
spent the day in a more quiet way.

James Stewart, resident of Council City (now Burlingame), wrote about attending the Independence Day celebration held on the Delaware River:

Osage County, K. T.
Wed., [July] 4, [1855]

Scattered Clouds, a few drops of rain but temperature pleasant. This is my first Fourth of July in Kansas. Dressed up in the morning, and went to the celebration ground. Being on committee of arrangement I went to work preparing for diner (a free diner) provisions having been prepared and brought by the Ladies in attendance, worked at this until the exercises of the day commenced, which consisted of music by the Choir, prayer by the Rev. Lowery, brief address and reading of Declaration of Independence by Edmund Fish Esq. An oration by Dr. Kerr, a Poem by M C Haven. Free collation & a multitude of toasts and host of other entertainments, after the assembly dispersed I came home by the boarding house and received two letters and some papers, am much pleased with this days experience. . . .

Joseph Savage, his brother, Forrest, and two cousins packed up their musical instruments in the fall of 1854, and, as part of the New England Emigrant Aid Company, departed the Hartford, Vermont, train station with Kansas Territory as their destination. The men settled in Lawrence and, together with others, formed the Lawrence Band. Although supportive of the antislavery movement taking root in Kansas, Joseph Savage had another reason to go: He wished to acquire land for a family farm, where he could continue growing apples and other fruit. Though originally interested in Wisconsin, he changed his mind while on a trip to Boston. The quick change of plans took him to Kansas.

After preparing his claim in Lawrence, Joseph returned to Vermont for his wife, Amanda, and their four children. Initially excited about the new home, the family instead landed in Kansas City with heavy hearts, following the death of infant Charlie, who died en route. Determined to stay, the family settled in on the farm. Amanda did so against her parents' wishes, believing the cause of freedom gave her no choice. A few months later, she and her newborn child died. Joseph and his daughter, Susan, suffered more loss, when not long after, two more children perished. In 1858 Joseph remarried, according to good friend, Edward Fitch, in a letter to his parents. Joseph's interests in farming, geology, and playing music with the band continued. In 1879, the band played at the Old Settlers' Meeting in Bismarck Grove. The occasion celebrated the twenty-fifth anniversary of the settling of Lawrence. Though Joseph did not attend, another band member read his written account of the early band. Charles Robinson, former governor of Kansas, also fondly remembered the troupe and their role in the young community:

> We all remember how much they cheered us, all through the early days and how too, they mingled their notes with our sorrows in times of trouble. . . .

Through all of his joys and sorrows, Joseph held a steadfast affection for Kansas, where he lived until his death in 1891.

The Lawrence Band furnished music for the first Fourth of July celebration held in Lawrence in 1855. Joseph's friend, Edward

Fitch, later joined the band. During the next several years, the band added members and instruments, their music cheering many an event in Lawrence.

Sara Robinson also attended the July Fourth celebration in Lawrence in 1855, where the day's events included a speech by her husband, James, already a prominent figure in the Territory. She wrote about the day's excitement:

July 4th [1855]

The morning of the Fourth came in cloudy, yet pleasant. Word had been sent to the people on the Wakarusa, and many were expected. Invitations also were sent out to the Delaware and Shawnee Indians to mingle in our festivities. From the elevated position of our house we saw the people gathering from all quarters. Several teams, of oxen as well as horses, the roughness of the vehicles being hidden under garlands of green leaves and flowers, came in from the Wakarusa. A beautiful flag was presented by a Massachusetts lady to the military companies of Lawrence, in an appropriate speech, in behalf of the ladies of Lawrence.

After its acceptance, the procession formed upon Massachusetts street and was escorted by the military to a fine grove about a mile from town. Here, in one of Nature's grand old forests, seats had been provided, and a platform raised for the orators and other speakers, for the singers and musical instruments. The number present was variously estimated from

fifteen hundred to two thousand. It was a motley gathering. There were many people with eastern dress and manner, and settlers from Missouri, and other far western states, no less distinctly marked by theirs. The Delawares and Shawnees added no little to the interest of the occasion. After the reading of the Declaration of Independence, whose embodied truths seemed to have gained new vitality, new force, since we last listened to it, came the oration. . . .

Chestina Bowker Allen and her family attended holiday activities in the Manhattan area, and later recorded the experiences in her diary:

July 4th [1855]
Independence Day passed away quietly.
A picnic at Manhattan and a dinner at
Mrs. Dyer's to which we were all invited.

July 4th [1857]
All our family, in the company with the
Williston family, old acquaintances
who had just arrived from Mass. Go to
a picnic just beyond Manhattan. Spent

the day pleasantly, had a good dinner, about 300 people present. Speeches, sentiments, singing, renewing old acquaintances and forming new were the features of the day

Samuel Reader of Indianola, near Topeka, did not attend any ceremonies, but wrote about how he spent the Fourth of July:

Friday, 4 [July 1856]
Warm clear Cooler than Thur. A number of Cannon fired at Topeka – I think there will be no war at all (pshaw on it all) . . . I feel better Spirits. No war. I got berries. Swam in river. Water chard. Cannon shots p.m. I play the fiddle.

Walter Hastings Woods lived in Kansas Territory during 1858 and 1859. He and his associates opened a wagon shop in Sumner, Atchison County. In his diary entry for Independence Day, he wrote about holiday festivities in Sumner:

Monday, July 4, 1859
It is a lovely day. We have a celebration in Sumner to day. I went up to the grove in the forenoon and a ball in the evening at the Sumner House. Moses went with me. I had a good time with Gray Hull.

As writer William Tomlinson continued his travels through the Territory, he made sure to stop and observe celebrations of the Fourth:

The settlers in the vicinity of Sugar Mound selected the Mound itself as the place for their convocation, and on the very ground where Gen. Clarke encamped his men in '56, the assembled settlers commemorated the anniversary of our country's liberty, and rejoiced in the triumph of the principles of their forefathers on the disputed soil of Kansas. The Fourth coming on the Sabbath, the citizens of Linn Co. held their celebration the third, and the day being favorable, several hundreds of the inhabitants of Linn and adjoining counties were in attendance. . . .

Tomlinson went on to describe Independence Day events in neighboring Raysville, Bourbon County, that he thought "greatly eclipsed" those in Sumner:

The patriotism, which inspired the settlers of the Osage during the gloomy period of their history, strikingly manifested itself in the double celebration of the time-honored principles of their fathers and their own deliverance from long-endured tyranny.

Early on the morning of July 5th, the slumbers of the good citizens of the Little Osage were suddenly broken by some of the already assembled freemen on the ground of the celebration, who were giving vent to their patriotism by firing a national salute from a small cannon they had secured for the occasion. The sun had scarcely risen above the green slopes of the prairie, when in every direction might be seen the beauty and strength of Northern Bourbon Co., coming on horse-back and in wagons, to celebrate the anniversary of our country's liberty. . . .

Nothing occurred to mar the harmony of the proceedings or cast the least shadow of gloom over the day's festivities. Numbers were in attendance from distant parts of the Territory and Western Missouri, and in all the number of people assembled could not have been much less than a thousand. . . .

Weddings gave settlers another reason to celebrate, and made up just one aspect of Samuel Adair's ministries during his life in Kansas. Reverend Adair traveled to Kansas in 1855 with support from the American Missionary Association. He began his ministerial journey in Ohio, where he attended college and seminary at

Oberlin College, graduating in 1841. Samuel and his wife, Fiorella, a half-sister of abolitionist John Brown, traveled to Osawatomie in 1854, after serving churches in Michigan and Ohio for several years. The couple settled on a claim near Osawatomie in 1855. Reverend Adair's sermon diary shows he began preaching in Council City (now Burlingame) in 1855. He also gave sermons in Osawatomie, Pottawatomie, and Lawrence, often speaking in parishioners' homes. Later, in 1855, he established the Congregational Church in Osawatomie. Many settlers mention Adair in their diaries. As a known abolitionist, Adair provided a great deal of support to the free-state movement in the Territory, including sheltering John Brown on several occasions. He worked hard at soliciting and distributing financial aid from various societies in the East. In addition, he distributed clothing and other supplies that came to settlers by way of groups such as the National Kansas Committee in New England, the Ladies Aid Society, and the Free Mission Sewing Society of the First Congregational Church. His diary and letters show his commitment to the struggling settlers of the area, offering constant hope and support.

In 1865, Fiorella Adair died in Leavenworth, where Reverend Adair served as a chaplain during the Civil War. Following his wife's death, Samuel returned to Osawatomie, where he died in 1898.

In addition to his diary, Adair kept a record of the marriages he performed. Weddings took place throughout the year, including these in the summers of 1856–1858:

1856 Record of Marriages –
No. 24 In Osawatomie, Lykins Co. Territory of Kansas, Mr.
Jeremiah Harrison and Elizabeth Kirkland were joined together in
Marriage by me on the 15th day of June A.D. 1856.
  S.L. Adair
  Minister – Gospel

1858 Record of Marriages –

No. 33. Osawatomie, Territory of Kansas, Eli Perkins and
Elizabeth Clementing Seymour were joined together in Marriage
by me, on the 3rd day of July, A.D. 1858.

    S.L. Adair
    Minister – Gospel

1858 Record of Marriages –

No. 34. At the house of Philander Bishop in Osawatomie, Territory
of Kansas, Cyrus Tator & Mary E. Bishop were joined together in
Marriage by me on the 5th day of July, A.D. 1858.

    S.L. Adair
    Minister – Gospel

No. 35. At my own house in Osawatomie, Lykins Co. Territory of
Kansas, on the 4th day of August A.D. 1858, Peter McMullen &
Nancy Sailing were joined together in Marriage by me.

    S.L. Adair
    Minister – Gospel

Thomas Wells and others gave accounts of weddings in their diaries and in letters home:

Juniata, Kanzas T.
Aug. 29, [1855]
Mrs. Thomas P. Wells

My Dear Mother,
I have neglected writing to you for some time past, waiting to receive a letter from you first, but it does not come and I will put off writing no longer. . . .
We had a wedding here last week out of doors! One of Mr. Hanna's daughters was married to a Mr. Dyer who lives at Juniata about four miles from here, he is a son of the old man Dyer who is spoken of in Boynton's "Journey through Kanzas" which you saw while I was at home. The knot was tied at four o'clock last Thursday evening.

A long table was set under the trees, loaded with cakes of various kinds, tarts made from native grapes, which by the way are much smaller than the wild grapes of the east, custards, preserves etc., while at a side table was roast pork, mutton and chicken in abundance. At about three o'clock the bridegroom and his friends with the "preacher" came a part in two large two horse wagons and others on horseback. The bridegroom was dressed in

*black coat and pants with white vest and the bride in pure white
with a head dress also of white. At the appointed hour the relations
and friends formed a semicircle; the bride and bridegroom stood
up alone in front and the minister before them. After they had
promised to love, respect, obey, etc., as long as they both should
live they were pronounced man and wife. After dinner all were
invited to the "infare" or second wedding at the house of Mr. Dyer
on the morrow. . . .*

Wells continued to describe the events:

*On the next morning I had the pleasure of riding down with them
to the infare where we remained until nearly night. This time
the table was set in a large log house, a story and a half high,*

containing four rooms with a kitchen built on one side, this is a first class house in Kansas.

We were supplied with a great variety of nice things than we had the day before. More than fifty persons were there to take dinner with them.

After dinner some of the company took a walk to the water melon patch, eat as many as they wished and went back loaded with melons for those that they had left behind. We had no dancing, no instrumental music but considerable time was spent in singing sacred songs. So you have a brief description of a wedding in Kanzas. . . .

Love to all,
Yours affectionately
T. C. Wells

Chestina Bowker Allen wrote about attending the same wedding:

Aug 23rd [1855]
Most of the family go to a dinner party, an infair or wedding feast of William Dyer and Miss Jane Hanna.
Chestina Bowker Allen
From her diary

Melissa Genett Anderson arrived in Kansas Territory at age twelve with her mother and six brothers and sisters. By the time the family made it to Coffey County in November 1857, her father had already built a log house on their claim, having arrived months earlier. Friend of the family, Phillip Marshall Moore, traveled to Kansas with the Andersons and lived with them for a short time before taking a claim in nearby Woodson County. He and Melissa became close friends and married when Melissa was fifteen years old and Phillip twenty-four.

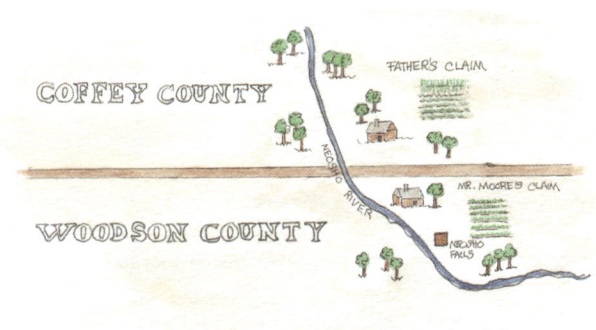

August the tenth was approaching but, consulting the almanac, we found that the tenth came on Friday. So my wedding was postponed two days. On Sunday, August 12, 1860, in our little box house on the farm, I was married to Philip Marshall Moore. My husband's claim was a timbered one on the Neosho River. It was in Woodson County, two and one-half miles from Neosho Falls, and three miles from Father's first claim in Coffey County. . . .

Entertainment

It must have been quite a sight to see the colorful wagons and exotic animals of Mabie's Circus as they crossed the prairie on their way to Topeka, Kansas Territory, in July 1859. The "newly organized menagerie and circus" gave two shows that day, following a parade through the city. Adults paid fifty cents for admission, children, twenty-five cents.

An illustrated advertisement from the June 23 edition of the *Topeka Tribune* promised "feats of posturing and leaping," cannonball exploits, and "feats of strength by the Herculean Artist." Professor Beagley was to "enter the den of Lions, Tigers, and Leopards," providing "a terrific contact with wild beasts." A brass and string band provided accompaniment.

On July 7, 1859, the *Topeka Tribune* provided a few lines on the day of the big event:

THE SHOW. This, Wednesday morning, crowds are coming to see the Elephant. From present appearances we are to have a big crowd in town today.

A few days later, the *Tribune* published a short observation of the circus:

Mabie's Circus
The great day for the boys, above all the other days of the year, is that on which the circus comes. The great pictures posted on all the available corners; of men in all positions but a natural one; of horses leaping through hoops; of monkies and elephants and camels and lions, are a two week's wonder. And when at last the great day comes it is quite equal to a theatre to see them.

Though the circus moved on, settlers found many other ways to enjoy themselves:

Sumner, Kansas Territory
Saturday, 26 [June 1858]
Was a very hot day. A party of ladies and gentlemen came down from Leavenworth and had a dance at the Sumner House in the evening.

Wednesday, 30 [June 1858]
A very hot day. Marcus J. Parrot, and 30 others came from
Leavenworth. We had a barbaque. Parrot made a speech and a
ball in the evening.
    Walter Hastings Woods
    From his diary

George Hildt arrived in Kansas Territory with his friend Charles Wood in June 1857 from Canal Dover, Ohio. Hildt and Wood started a community in southern Johnson County, where other Ohioans later joined them, including one, William Quantrill, who would later become infamous as the leader of a raid on Lawrence in 1856. In January 1858, Hildt left Kansas. During the Civil War he fought with the Thirtieth Ohio Volunteer Infantry and participated in the 1861 battle at Antietam, Maryland. Though his diary covers only six months, Hildt's entries described everyday life in great detail:

Southern Johnson County, Kansas Territory
June 21, 1857
Sunday a very dull hot day a good deal of traveling on the road
a great many going to Paoli when the land sale goes off this week
Sunday evening we all felt in the humor for singing and Old
hundred Boylstin O for a thousand tongues
to sing Alass and did my savior Bleed &c
went forth on the prairie where no such
sounds were ever before uttered. The ox
goad and Haw Buck the braying of mules
cattle bells &c are much more common We
sang just as we felt and I need not tell that
we all thought of home we all conjecture
where we would pass the time were we in Dover & how much
rather we would be here with our present prospects than there
lounging round with nothing to make us exert ourselves.

The Topeka Tribune
June 2, 1859

Lectures

Professor Stark, is lecturing nightly, this week, at Museum Hall, drawing crowded houses on the subjects of Phrenology and Phisiology. His lectures on Tuesday and Wednesday evenings were free. For the remaining three nights of the week, he charges 50 cents admission. His gallery of paintings draws much attention. We bespeak for the Professor full houses during the remainder of his stay among us. He comes to us well recommended by the press. You cannot spend fifty cents to a better advantage than by patronizing Professor Stark.

The Herald of Freedom
Lawrence, Kansas Territory
July 18, 1857

The New England Bards

This incomparable troupe, now making a tour of Kansas, have arrived in the Territory, and gave one of their amusing and instructive entertainments at the Unitarian Church on Wednesday evening, the 15th inst. M. Durant, director of the Bards, was musical director of Ossian E. Dodge's late concert troupe. Their happy efforts last Tuesday evening, on the balcony of the Morrow House, is a sufficient guaranty to all who heard them, of the excellence of their music. This being the first visit of any musical troupe to the West, we bespeak for them a welcome such as the pioneers of Kansas only know how to give. One of their songs is descriptive of, and entitled "Kansas Emigration", which is sung by the Bards with excellent effect.

Kansas soon our home shall be,
Where land is cheap and water free.
The streams are over-run with fish,
And they dip 'em up with a handled dish.
Go and see them. "A word to the wise is sufficient."

The Herald of Freedom
August 8, 1857

Sewing Circle

The ladies of the Lawrence Sewing Circle held a festival at the Plymouth Congregational Church, on Thursday evening of last week, for the purpose of raising funds to furnish the same. The attendance was very good, and the entertainment satisfactory. There was a splendid supper, and good music by the band and by amateur performers. The party broke up, after enjoying themselves to a late hour.

The Kanzas News
July 25, 1857
Emporia, Linn County

A "Loafer's Club" has been organized in Emporia which promises to be very successful. The rules of the club are very rigid. One of them is to the effect that any member guilty of sweating will be fined—a repetition of the offence is punished by compelling the guilty one to walk thirty steps in the sun, without stopping or assistance.

Personal Pursuits

With the day's work completed, settlers looked for respite from the heat to read, or, like Samuel Reader, to play music. Samuel mentions several instruments in his diary, including a clarinet, a flute, a fiddle, and an accordion:

Indianola, Kansas Territory
Sat. [July] 30, [1855]
Clear I set out posts for the maison; fixed it up. PM. went for berries
Got few. Came home. Made a jug of clay; burnt it. Cool. I played
flute at night to soothe the Indians and neighbors. Silver Moon!

Sun. [July] 5, [1857]
Warm I read We live in Chambra Co. I read Shakespeare . . .
Invited to ball, played flute.
    Samuel J. Reader
    From his diary

Council City, Kansas Territory
SAT. [July] 21 [1855]
Cloudy & rainy nearly all day, rained some last night. Lay back &
read most the day, finished reading Cowpers task and commenced
Gertrude of Wyoming, went down to Hoovers in the afternoon,
then to Freels & paid for some flour, came back home past Hoovers
and got a loaf of bread.

SUN. [July] 22 [1855]
Warm with broken clouds. Lay back & read, had a call from Mr
Mcdonald & Plumb. Mcdonald stayed all night finished reading
Gertrude of Wyoming, had a great deal of talk with Mr Mcdonald
on religion and other things.

TUES. [July] 31 [1855]
Terific thunder & lightning and a fine shower last night, Clear
pleasant with a fine breeze . . . Came home went down to Freels,
thence to Brattons, thence to Hoovers, took supper there, thence
home, sang, fiddled on three strings, read wrote & went to bed.
  James Stewart
  From his diary

Sumner, Atchison County
Friday, [August] 6, [1858]
A very hot day. I am reading the first book of Caesar now.
  Walter Hastings Woods
  From his diary

Reading books provided enjoyment, but reading letters from faraway friends and family brought the familiar and a rekindling of spirit. With pen in hand, answering letters gave the opportunity to share news and loving thoughts.

James Sayre Griffing's westward adventure started in Indianapolis, Indiana, where he began his career as a pastor, organizing a Sunday school and building a church in the spring and summer of 1854. Just as Griffing completed the church roof, Reverend William Goode, a Methodist pastor who had visited Kansas shortly after the Kansas–Nebraska Act was passed, called on Griffing and recruited him for service in Kansas Territory.

After arriving in November 1854, Reverend Griffing went on to Wakarusa Mission, the base for his circuit ministry. For the next year, the young pastor and his pony, Jacob, covered many miles, visiting settlers and organizing Sunday school classes.

In 1855, James traveled home to New York to marry his sweetheart, Augusta Goodrich. The couple then returned to Kansas to live on their farm, located east of Topeka. James and Augusta had four children, John, William, Mary, and Sarah, the latter dying as a young child. James continued his Methodist ministry for twenty-five years, spending his final years leading an African-American congregation in Manhattan. During this time, James served as an agent of the Freedmen's Bureau, and, true to character, helped many members who had been former slaves. In 1882, James died at the age of fifty-nine, from the effects of malaria, a disease he had first contracted shortly after coming to Kansas. The sickness took a toll on him, and he never quite regained the strength he'd had when he arrived. Through it all, he continued his life of preaching and helping his fellow citizens.

Reverend Joseph Denison, a longtime colleague of James, wrote these words, published in the Methodist Annual Conference Meeting Minutes, in tribute to his friend:

As a professing Christian, a preacher, a pastor, a husband, a father, a friend, a citizen, he was emphatically a good man and full of faith and of the Holy Ghost, and while his departure makes one less in the church militant, it makes one more in the church triumphant.

Augusta Griffing lived in Manhattan until her death in 1906. She and James are buried in Sunset Cemetery in Manhattan.

From James's early days in Indianapolis, he and Augusta shared thoughts and news in their letters. James kept Augusta informed on his circuit adventures, and Augusta wrote of family and events in New York, including her trip back to Owego in 1859. James also wrote to Augusta during her absence:

Topeka, Aug. 7th 1859

Dear Cutie,

I went to town Friday morning expecting I should get another letter from you from home, but it came not. Saturday evening I walked over to Br Curtis, to see if one had come and still none, he said I looked disappointed, but I am sure I could not have looked worse than I felt . . .

And now Cutie, I only wish I was with you to day, and could see yourself, and my darling boy. How have you been, and who all have you seen and do you get any stronger than when you left. Is Johnny a good boy, be careful not to let him have his own head and way too much, a little discipline and care now will be worth more than a great deal by and by. Is he kind & affectionate still and do you suppose he would know me. Has he been sick any since he left? And have you? Have you visited my mother yet? And does she look as healthy as when we left. Has she seemed to grow old fast? I wish you would write quite often. I don't think I ever was so glad to get letters. I wish I could get one every time I get mail from the office, which is two or three times a week. How many letters have you received from me? . . .

Hug darling for papa. Keep well dear.

Write soon.

Your own husband James

> *Lawrence, Kansas Territory*
> *July 15, [1855]*
> *Last Thursday I got two letters one*
> *from you and one from Roline. These*
> *letters give me new life. How my*
> *heart leaps with pleasing sensations*
> *when I recognize the well known*
> *handwriting, yours. I opened first*
> *and examined every letter minutely,*
> *held it in every possible shape resting*
> *in good faith that I could read your*
> *innermost thoughts. . . .*
> *Frank Mayo in a letter to his*
> *wife, Thankful,*
> *who was to arrive in the fall*

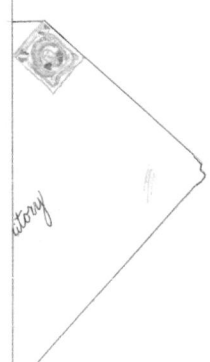

Osawatomie, K. T.
July 11, 1856

Dear Cousin Melinda:
. . . I write this with baby in lap, holding book on my knee. I hope
that you will enjoy the reading as much as I do the writing. I often
wish that I could monopolize a telegraph. I would often hold
converse with my dear friends in Watertown; but with children in
my lap and at my elbows, I find little time for correspondence. . . .
Write soon. Write all the news,
Jane Carruth

Thoughts on Kansas

Lawrence K. T. (Sumner Terrace)
June 21 [1857]

*It is Sunday–The cares & toils of the week are suspended. I have
leisure to read & write & think . . . I can say truly that I like Kansas
I like this mode of life. It is fresh–every night when, after tea I
seat myself at the door–I think over those olden Bible times when
Abraham sat at the door of his tent. I look south & East and see the
broad, green & beautiful acres which I call mine–There is a dilation
of soul when one looks abroad upon the prairies, fresh as from the
hands of their maker. It seems as though one might begin life anew;
he casts off the old slough of a former civilization & Enters upon
an untried life. He feels that he can make it fairer and better. That
he can work up things somewhat after his own mind. That he can
make his farm more productive & pleasanter to look upon.*
 John Stillman Brown
 In a letter to his son, William

Autumn

Our corn is much higher than we can reach – it is earring out, our pumpkins and squashes are for the most part fruiting well and we have one large patch of beans that promise well. Our tomatoes are getting on as fast as they can but will not be ripe under a fortnight. Those with a few hills of potatoes comprise all our crop this year. Our cabin is still in a dilapidated condition – our sickness preventing us from fixing it up. The rain and sunshine of heaven can both alike visit us, but we murmur not at either – why should we murmur at anything that comes from Heaven.

Sarah Everett
September 1, 1855
From a letter to her sister

After the passage of the Kansas–Nebraska Act in May 1854, prospective Kansans wasted no time in preparing and packing up for Kansas Territory. By fall of that year, Lawrence, Topeka, Leavenworth, and Atchison had been founded. Autumn arrivals—including Joseph Savage, Lewis Litchfield, and Cyrus K. Holliday—helped these settlements grow from tents to towns. One enthusiastic emigrant, Robert Gilbert, made an even longer journey to pursue his dreams in the West. He sailed from London, England, on September 6, 1855, and was so eager to be a part of the American westward expansion that, upon arrival in New York, he renounced his English citizenship and traveled to Lawrence, where he settled on a farm north of town.

The months of September and October found farmers in the Territory harvesting corn, squash, pumpkins, and other vegetables. Although some 1856 crops had suffered, Thomas Wells still expected to have a good harvest of vegetables, as he reported to his parents. Peter Bryant, who farmed in Holton, Kansas, wrote to his brother about the abundance of fruit and vegetables he had in a September 1859 letter, saying, "We live pretty high now. We have taters, beans, tomatoes, corn dodgers, and all the melons we want to roll in. . . ." If a farmer's harvest did not include onions, wild onions could be sub- stituted, "which prove very acceptable to the Settler to give him a zest or relish to other kind of food . . ." This flavorful advice came courtesy of Robert Tovey in his narrative on practical life in Kansas.

Livestock also needed food, and dry autumn days provided ideal conditions for cutting hay. The hay would be cut with a scythe, allowed to dry on one side, then "teddered," or turned over, to dry on the other side. Then the hay would be raked into shocks, or conical stacks, to dry for another few days. Walter Woods of Sumner men- tioned helping his neighbor, Parker, with his hay in September 1858. Peter Bryant wrote to his brother that he had already cut sixteen tons and expected to cut more.

September weather could be dry, but it could also be very warm. Edward Fitch, in a September 8, 1855, letter to his parents, wrote that it had been so hot the day before, "large hard apples laid on a bench at the east end of our store baked almost through . . ." He added that "such days are uncommon, though Sept. is our hottest month here." In Indianola, later that month, Samuel Reader cut waist-high grass and put the finishing touches on his chimney. The weather had started to cool off. By October 4, the temperatures had dropped dramatically, as Samuel noted in his diary. He would need that chimney. He pulled on his mittens, as a "hard cold N. wind and dreadful cold" had arrived. Winter would not be far behind.

Rain and sunshine both fell on Kansas, but not always in the needed amount. Following the droughts of 1856 and 1860, there were few crops to harvest. Settlers continued to receive aid through the fall from all over the country. Much of the relief came through the efforts of the New England Emigrant Aid Company. Generous supporters in the North and East, including women in Orange, New Jersey, responded to the Company's pleas for assistance, and donated food, clothing, and sewing materials. In 1860, James Blood of the National Kansas Committee coordinated relief offers of money, wheat, and potatoes from Illinois residents. Churches and individuals joined in the effort. In a letter from November 1856, Edward Fitch thanked his parents for sending barrels of clothing to be distributed to citizens in need. Lewis Bacon referred to "clothing from the [E]ast distributed to those in want in Lawrence," in a November 10, 1857, diary entry.

Although 1856 proved to be a challenging year both economically and politically, the atmosphere calmed after President Buchanan appointed John Geary of Pennsylvania to be Territorial governor in July. In reflecting on the political climate of the Territory in those first few years, Reverend Richard Cordley wrote about the many mass meetings and free-state gatherings held in Grasshopper Falls, Big Springs, and elsewhere. These were in addition to the more-formal conventions held in Lecompton and Wyandotte. Cordley added:

> It was a time, too, of intense excitement, and consequently of intense impressions. Ideas come to stay when they come to men in such a condition. Three such years would do more to mark a people for their own than three score of ordinary years. Kansas still bears the marks of those early days. It was in those times of upheaval and of intense impression that Kansas received her form and spirit. . . .

In October 1859, after years of various debates and documents, settlers voted on and approved the Wyandotte Constitution, drawn up by the constitutional convention that had taken place in July. The document would become the state constitution when Kansas entered the Union in January 1861.

Impending statehood gave citizens a reason to be thankful in the fall of 1860. No matter the challenges they had faced through the year, settlers took time not only for a special day of thanks, but also to enjoy a good book, a joyful song, or each other's company.

Emigration

Deeply influenced by his Quaker background, poet John Greenleaf Whittier exemplified the principles of compassion and social responsibility through his writing and political activities. In 1831, he published his first book of prose and verse, *Legends of New England*. A passionate critic of slavery, Whittier wrote extensively on the subject that he referred to as the "national crime." To show support for the antislavery cause in Kansas Territory, he wrote "The Kansas Emigrant Song" in 1854. The words, sung to the tune of "Auld Lang Syne," inspired the second party of the New England Emigrant Aid Company as they left New England in the late summer of 1854.

The Kanzas Emigrant Song
J. G. Whittier

We cross the prairie as of old,
The pilgrims crossed the sea,
To make the West, as they the East,
The homestead of the free.

We go to rear a wall of men
On Freedom's Southern line,
And plant beside the cotton tree,
The rugged Northern pine!

We're flowing from our native hills
As our free rivers flow;
The blessing of our motherland
Is on us as we go.

We go to plant her common schools
On distant prairie swells,
And give the Sabbaths of the wild
The music of her bells.

Upbearing, like the ark of old,
The Bible in our van,
We go to test the truth of God
Against the fraud of man.

No pause, nor rest, save where the streams
That feed the Kansas run,
Save where our Pilgrim gonfalon
Shall flout the setting sun!

We'll sweep the prairie as of old
Our fathers swept the sea,
And make the West, as they the East,
The homestead of the free!

Joseph Savage, from Vermont, witnessed the exciting send-off. He described the event in his *Recollections of 1854*:

> *At Boston a large crowd gathered at the depot to see the second party off for Kansas. The great American poet, J. G. Whittier, had written a poem expressly for us. It was printed on nice large cards and distributed freely among the crowd, and a request given by Dr. Webb for all to join in the song, which they did in good earnest. It was set to Auld Lang Syne. We played the tune over once on our instruments, and then the song was sung by many with tears in their eyes. The song was worthy of a poet and the occasion, and should be written in letters of gold, or chiseled in the solid marble on the monument which will some day be here erected to freedom. We sang this song on our weary march across the Shawnee reserve, around our camp fires, and in the lonely tent on the town site; it was the inspiring sentiment in the hearts of those who dared to brave all for freedom, and thus forever consecrate these hills and valleys to her children.*

Lewis Timothy Litchfield also waited at the depot that day, traveling with his wife, Anna, and another Litchfield, possibly his father. Lewis, from Cambridge, Massachusetts, looked forward to new opportunities in the West. Once in Lawrence, Lewis and Anna opened the first "hotel" on September 25, 1854. Early residents gave the large, tent-like structure the nickname "Astor House." Litchfield remained in Kansas until June 3, 1861, when he enlisted in Company D, Kansas First Infantry Regiment. Only two months later, he died at Wilson's Creek, Missouri, and is buried at Oak

Hill Cemetery in Lawrence. In beautiful script, Litchfield gave an account of his departure from Boston:

> *It was a beautiful day, the 29th day of August, 1854. The sun shone brightly in the heavens and the hot summer air was already giving [way] to the cool pleasant breezes of Autumn. . . .*
>
> *We are there in assembly of about two hundred persons old and young, some gay and joyous, others sad and weeping. . . .*

Savage and Litchfield both later described the Lawrence town site as it first appeared:

> *About two o'clock in the afternoon on the 16th of September, 1854, we arrived on Mount Oread. . . . Soon our teams came up, and we drove down on the town site, and pitched our tents nearly in front of where the jail now stands. This was the first Yankee tent, and our first night, on the then to be great city of Lawrence.*
>
> *Before pitching our tents for the night, we, like pilgrims at the end of their journey, went for the first time to bath our wearied limbs in the turbid waters of the Kaw. As we first cast our longing eyes over its surface, and felt the cooling embrace of its waters, a feeling of ownership and affection sprang up in our hearts, for on its banks were soon to be our homes . . . The tall oak, elm and cottonwood then spread out their long branches defiantly to the noonday sun, while beneath their shade the silence of nature reigned supreme.*
>
> *We ate our first meal on the town site, from the scanty stores left of bread, cheese and dried meat, which had been so carefully packed by our wives and mothers, in our Eastern homes. . . .*
>
> *Joseph Savage*
> In Recollections of 1854

*"First city of Kansas" junction of the Wakarusa
and Kansas river, then 5 miles upriver,
Kansas Territory.*

*Here we were in the place which we
were to call our home, no house in sight,
and the boundless prairie only before,
behind, and on our left. The noble
Kansas rolled on our right. It was truly a
lovely place. The prairie extends boldly up to
the river with an elevation of about thirty feet.
To the west of us was a high bluff from summit
could be seen the country for miles around us. . . .*

*. . . A city had sprung up where ten months
ago the prairie hens had built their nests and reared their
young for centuries. . . . Soon numerous campfires could be seen
blazing in front of each tent throwing a cheerful radiance around.
All seemed happy in their new situation, and thus was founded
the first city in Kansas Territory. . . . The evenings were spent
around a large fire, while pleasant conversation and stories of bold
adventure helped pass the time very pleasantly. The hearty laugh
might be heard for a great distance on the prairie silencing for a
time the loud and piercing howl of the prairie wolf.*

Lewis Timothy Litchfield
From his diary

A few weeks later, Cyrus K. Holliday arrived in Lawrence. Born
in Carlisle, Pennsylvania, in 1826, Holliday attended Allegheny
College in Meadville and graduated in 1852. As a young man, he
involved himself in several business ventures, in particular a successful local railroad line. He married Mary Dillon Jones in 1854,
and later that year left for Kansas. After spending two months in
Lawrence, Holliday wrote to his wife, "I am now 30 miles above
Lawrence on the Kansas River, assisting in starting a new town."

Holliday founded, and became president of, the Topeka Town Company. Mary and the couple's two children, Lillie and Charles, joined him later, after political violence had subsided.

At the Wyandotte Constitutional Convention in July 1859, Holliday successfully lobbied for Topeka to become the future state capital. That same year he served the first of many terms as the town's mayor. Remaining involved in state and local politics, Holliday served in both the Territorial and state legislatures. In 1868, after years of planning and building, Holliday finally broke ground on his major project, the Atchison, Topeka, and the Santa Fe Railroad. Cyrus Holliday died in 1900 and is buried in Topeka Cemetery. Shortly after his arrival in Lawrence in October 1854, Holliday shared his first impressions of the area with Mary:

City of Lawrence, K. T.
Nov. 18, [1854]

My Dear Mary –
Through the politeness of the City Magistrate I am favored with material to pen you a single line just previous to Mr Ingrams departure – Had it not been for his kindness you could not have heard from me except by word of mouth.
    . . . I am perfectly delighted with the country – You may tell those who inquire that my idea of the country is simply this – that God might have made a better country than the Kansas but so far as my knowledge extends he certainly never did. . . .
    Ingram will tell you how to address me & I hope to hear from you often – much oftener than you can hear from me. . . .
    Remember, Mary, that I am your Husband – that you are my wife – that as such I love you fondly and most dearly –
    A letter from you will do me much good –
    Yours affectionately
    Holliday

After being separated from her husband, Frank, for several months, Thankful Cobb Mayo described her anticipation as she approached Kansas City on the steamboat *Polar Star* to meet him:

> *Thursday, September 16th 1855*
> *Can it indeed be Thankful Cobb, on board of a steamboat on the Missouri River, so many, many weary miles from home and parents? I can scarcely realize my own identity. Thank God, that although the boat every hour is bearing me farther from my parents, I am drawing nearer my husband, that husband from whom I have been parted such a cruel length of time.*
> *Thankful Sophia Cobb Mayo*
> *From her diary*

In 1888, Thankful looked back and wrote sentimentally about her arrival in Kansas and the couple's new home:

> *I have been looking back trying to decide when I was the happiest, really, consciously superlatively happy . . . I think I stood for a while in the Elysian heights when I met Frank at Kansas City, Mo. In order to enjoy it seems to me we must first suffer. And I had suffered any amount of worry and anxiety during the six months*

of separation. He had seemed to me as far away in Kansas, as if he had gone to the moon . . . I had plenty of time to imagine all sort of calamities, and I had faithfully improved it. I had been filled with dismay at not finding him there on my arrival; but the morrow brought him and though he looked worn and haggard with hard work & poor fare I was happy. I still cherish the dress of yellow striped muslin that I wore on that glad day. . . .

. . . I smiled out from under the awning stretched over the one horse wagon as happy as Tennyson's princess for my husband was driver and we were bound for the promised land to set up our household goods (laughably few they were) in the bosom of the virgin prairie – the prairie about which I had read and dreamed so much. What though the awning refused to stay up, and the ardent rays of the mid September sun beat full upon my head and I sighed for a draught from a crystal spring, what were little discomforts to us whose path was love lit, invested with the glamour of romance and adventure. Ah! We were young!

Emigration into the Territory continued each autumn when weather, available water, and grass for livestock made traveling more feasible than in the summer. Newspapers carried articles on the anticipated arrivals, letters home carried loving words and accounts of the journeys, and diaries held recorded descriptions of scenery and fellow travelers:

Emporia, Linn County
The Kanzas News
September 26, 1857

Emigration

The fall "covered wagon" emigration has commenced in earnest. As we write, a long train of emigrant wagons, filled with "household angels" and "plunder" and accompanied by herds of cattle, is approaching from the East. These sights are of daily occurrence. Standing in the "gateway" of Southern and South-western Kanzas, we welcome the hardy pioneer to their rich valleys, and call upon the thousands coming to Kanzas to "take possession of the goodly land". Broad and fertile fields are awaiting the touch of the husbandman to make them "bloom and blossom as the rose". Beautiful and picturesque valleys, grand rolling prairies, underlaid with immense beds of stone and coal, and skirted by large belts of timber, are lying vacant, beckoning the hardy pioneer to "come and occupy". And they are coming! From New England, Ohio, Indiana, and all the Western States, they come! A conquering army without banners, an army of liberty-loving pioneers! Kanzas welcomes them. The prairies smile at their approach, "Thrice welcome".

After setting out on his second trip to Kansas in September 1857, Joseph Trego wrote to his wife, Alice, about missing her and their young daughters:

Sunday Afternoon on board the S. B. I. H. Oglesby
Missouri River, 12 miles Below Kansas City
[September 1857]

Dear Alice,
. . . There has been nothing of particular interest since we left St. Louis. I have endeavoured to make the time seem short by reading novels, but having nothing in the way of business or otherwise to

claim my attention I could but think of that which was the nearest to my mind's heart; home–My angel of a wife and our dear little girls. Oh! You don't know–maybe you do tho'–what a satisfaction, a delight it has been to me to have your miniature to look at, and Alice a tale which I read caused me to feel, for several days, a painful anxiety for your safety . . . I always felt proud of your spirit but I want you to wait until I get home again before you indulge too much of it . . . No more at present, so good bye love until we get to Sugar Mound.

> *With love to all I am*
> *Yours always Jo*
> *Kiss the children for me*

On August 17, 1858, at age twenty, Anna Watson Randolph left Ohio behind and, with her family, headed west for Kansas. Though the first leg of the journey passed somewhat slowly, as the riverboat they were on ran aground several times, Anna and her family made it safely to the Territory and settled in Emporia. In her diary, Anna described daily activities as well as some of her neighbors. She married Joseph Randolph on December 22, 1860. As she neared her new home, Anna recorded her impressions:

Between Burlingame and Emporia, Kansas Territory
September 12, 1858

We started out very early without breakfast. We stopped later for breakfast on the banks of the loveliest stream I ever saw, bright, beautiful shells–a perfect island of them. It is all Indian territory here. We expect to reach Emporia tonight.

> *Anna Margaret Randolph*
> *From her diary*

Lawrence, Kansas Territory
September 4th [1855]
Emigration again begins to pour into the territory. During the
last two months there has been little in this part of the country.
Cholera has raged on the river, and summer heats have been
too great for any comfort in travelling; but now the prairies
are again dotted with white-covered wagons of the western
emigrant. They come bringing everything with them in their
wagons, their furniture, provisions, and their families. Their
stock, also, is driven with the teams. Their wagons to them
are a travelling home; many of them having a stove set, with
pipe running through the top. They often travel far into the
territory; it matters to them little how far, so that they get a
location which pleases them. Then they build a cabin, and, with
a fixed habitation, they will become the strength and sinew of
the country. Being used to the emergencies and the hardships
of pioneer life, Kansas will depend upon them mostly, in this
early settlement, for the ground work, the substratum, upon
which to build up a most glorious new state. While they, for
the most part, settle in the country, and will gather into their
garners of the golden treasures of the rich and fertile soil,
eastern capital will form a nucleus, around which the young,
the adventurous, the enterprising, will gather, and new cities,
new towns, will spring up with rapid growth, emulating in thrift
and intelligence those of the old states.
   Sara Robinson
   From Kansas: Its Interior and Exterior Life

The Natural World

In each season, diary entries, especially those of male settlers, began with a very brief note about the weather. Cool. Cloudy. Clear. In autumn, the weather and the glowing landscape inspired some writers to give a more descriptive report:

Lawrence, Kansas Territory
Herald of Freedom
September 19, 1857
The weather at the present time is very like the hazy Indian Summer of the far East. Look to which point of the compass you will, and everywhere is presented a fair landscape o'erhung with Autumn's mellowness, and rich in hue and more than artistic coloring. These are not melancholy days, but the most beautiful of the seasons' children.

In the autumn of 1854, Reverend Charles B. Boynton and T. B. Mason made an extensive tour of Kansas Territory, after being commissioned by the "American Reform Tract and Book Society" and The Kansas League of Cincinnati, Ohio. Their task, as described in the preface, was "to explore and report upon the climate, soil, production and general resources, and promise of Kansas." Boynton and Mason hoped that with the increased interest in Kansas Territory following the passage of the Kansas–Nebraska Act, their presentation of facts with descriptions and narrative would promote interest among readers. In 1855, the two published *Journey through Kansas*, a compilation of the information they had gathered.

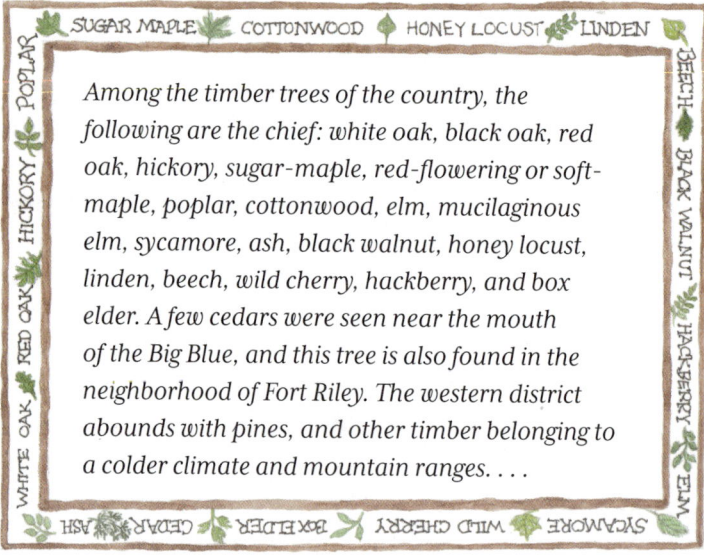

Among the timber trees of the country, the following are the chief: white oak, black oak, red oak, hickory, sugar-maple, red-flowering or soft-maple, poplar, cottonwood, elm, mucilaginous elm, sycamore, ash, black walnut, honey locust, linden, beech, wild cherry, hackberry, and box elder. A few cedars were seen near the mouth of the Big Blue, and this tree is also found in the neighborhood of Fort Riley. The western district abounds with pines, and other timber belonging to a colder climate and mountain ranges. . . .

Several of the pioneers who traveled to and through Kansas Territory, including Robert Atkins Tovey, felt a responsibility to share their acquired knowledge and experience with others who were contemplating the daunting journey. Tovey emigrated to Kansas in October 1854 from Albany, New York. He settled on Pottawatomie Creek near Osawatomie. In the preface of his handwritten "guide," Tovey explained his reasons for compiling the document:

> . . . the first is that now the tide of emigration is commencing again to flow into Kansas wide Fertile & most beautiful territory it is of the greatest importance that those who are going forth with their wives & children their property yea their all on earth Should have all the information concerning the country to which they are making a Pilgrimage. . . .

Tovey listed twelve chapters in his booklet. Topics included local Indians, Territorial government, and natural features such as soil and timber.

> Among the noble trees of the West will stand foremost the gigantic Oak of an immense height & frequently 5-1/2 feet through of these kind of trees we find it very convenient to make shingles for our cabins next is the black Walnut which frequently grows very large . . . the Elm grows to a very large size & likewise the Slippery Elm to so useful for medicinal purposes the Sycamore with its variggated bark connecting the margin of the rivers – the Alder & Elder trees grow abundantly here & the coffeenut Tree the timber of which is of a most valuable character being very hard & having a grain very similar to Mahogany – Hackberry which is a very valuable wood for many purposes – the Cotton tree and Button wood tree grows to a great extent there is likewise here several plantations of Willows of different specimens I should have observed that there are various kinds of Oak. . . .
>
> From A Twelve Months Practical Life in Kansas Territory, Written by an Actual Settler

As a sawmill operator, Joseph Trego took particular note of the trees in the Sugar Mound area where he lived and worked. In the autumn of 1857, Trego saw more than potential cabin logs, and wrote about the vivid colors in his diary and in a letter to his wife, Alice:

> *October 24 S. Fair. Went down to creek to look about some. The groves are looking beautiful now and where the sugar Maple abounds, there bright colors of various shades, from bright red to bright yellow the scene presented is gorgeous & beautiful beyond description. The Little Sugar, above the falls, is like a canal, several feet deep and 4 to 6 rods wide, for near a mile up the stream. We shot some ducks and squirrils on the way. Looked out a place to build our houses and returned home by way of Mr Cannon's mellon field where we found some right good mellon which went off well while the sun shone hot enough for a day in June.*
> *Joseph Trego*
> *From his diary*

Sugar Mound, K. T., Log Cabin yet
Oct. 25th 1857

My Dear Wife
Have expected all day to write but was prevented by the coming in
of visitors or something else so that I could not get time and feel in
the mood until now.

The boys are up on the hammock asleep. I have just got thro'
with an ablution here by the fireside and feel lots better for it, and
now, when everything is still I can talk to you without interruption.
I have written you three letters and have received one and I have
been away now seven weeks, nearly. Are you enjoying yourself
so much that you can't think what a dreary – (it would not be if
you were here, for it is a beautiful place now when the trees are
rigged out in such showy colors, particularly the sugar-maples,
which rather predominates, the color of which is bright red &
yellow, and all the shades of admixture of the two, while the oaks
are brownish and hickory's pale green &c, everything, even to
a rainy day—now that I can be in the cabin and look at it from
the window-is pleasing to the eye) lonesome kind of life I have to
lead – I would feel lonesome anywhere without you – and all that
makes it endurable is the "getting ready" to live and the looking
forward to spring – what a long way off – when I expect to join you
again. After that time I hope there will be no separation again for
at least sixty years to come. But what a number of things might
occur between now and the opening of spring to blast my hopes of
the future. I wont 'borrow trouble' however . . . so a sweet goodbye
love and don't forget to write again this winter.

Yours most affectionately,
J.
Joseph Trego
From a letter to his wife, Alice

Harvest time meant hard work and hopes that there would be food enough to last through the winter, for settlers and stock. Anxious loved ones awaited news on the settlers' well-being. Thomas Wells and others reassured family and reported on fall crops:

Manhattan, K. T.

Oct. 19th 1856

My dear Mother

We very gladly received a letter from you last Friday. . . .
I expect to harvest my corn this week, I think I shall have 275
or 300 bushels, and I expect to get 25 or 30 bush. potatoes and
two or three bush of beans – we have gathered
two or three wagon loads of winter squashes
crooknecks etc and have quite a lot of beets
yet in the garden.

I wish you and father and little
Herbert were here to share some of
the good things with us, prairie
hens will be plenty; once in a
while we may get a wild turkey, or a
deer, and we can buy dry buffalo meat
of the Indians, but in the absence of all
these we have beef, and there is no beef
like that raised on the Kansas prairies. . . .

Come now make up your minds to come out here and bring
the Lyme folks with you . . . say by next June, send father out
west on an exploring expedition. The journey will do him good,
even if he should decide to go back and spend his days in R. I.
nothing would be lost, and I assure you we should be very glad
to see him. . . .

Love to friends and I hope you will write often and oblige
yours truly,

T. C. Wells

Osawatomie, Kansas Territory
Sept. 3rd [1858]
Spent most of the day at labor cutting up corn. Corn very heavy –
Far beyond any thing we have raised before since we came here. O
that we could be thankful as we ought for the abundance of good
things to eat & drink which God has given us!

> *Samuel Adair*
> *From his diary*

Lawrence, Kansas Territory
The Kansas Tribune
October 17, 1855

Some Pumpkins

A load of the largest Pumpkins we ever saw, were brought into
town last week by Mr. J. D. Herrington. They were raised on a
farm near Franklin. One of them measured 5 feet 9 inches in
circumference and weighed 106 lbs. The entire load were of nearly
the same size, and were sold at from $1.00 to $1.50 each. They are
called the Seven-Year Pumpkins, on account of their being capable
of preservation for a great length of time.

Allen County, Kansas Territory
In September, 1859, Father sold his high prairie claim and
bought a second bottom claim in Allen County between Iola
and Humboldt. It was three miles from Iola, the county seat
of Allen County. I bade good-bye to my fiancé and left for our
new location. I had no reason to change my mind, although I
met a goodly number of young people that winter and had a
good time.

Our new home was a box house, the boards running
perpendicular. Here we had a fine truck patch, containing
pumpkins, squashes, watermelons and turnips. We made good
use of these. Two loads of pumpkins were allowed to freeze.
They were soft when frozen, and were put into a press. The
juice obtained was boiled down to a syrup. Another load of
pumpkins had been put under a haystack where they could not
freeze. These were stewed and used to thicken the syrup, the
mixture being boiled in an old-fashioned copper kettle. This
made twenty gallons of fine butter. We also made watermelon
rind preserves by cooking the rinds in a syrup made from
the juice of the melons. The preserves and butter make good
substitutes for sugar. . . .

Melissa Genett Anderson
From The Story of a Kansas Pioneer

Sumner, Kansas Territory
Thursday, 6 October 1859
It is a lovely day. Henry went to Leavenworth to day on stage.
I went out and got some Black Walnuts, Paw Paw, and Coffee
Bean leaves.

Walter Hastings Woods
From his diary

During C. B. Boynton's expedition through Kansas, a young member of the group, after documenting various natural features, turned his attention to the evening sky and wrote beautifully on his observations:

All day we had traveled amid scenes of wonderful beauty. We journeyed toward the setting sun, and often ere he sank into the plain, he drew our eyes to where the lengthening shadows, stretching away from every rock, and knoll, and tree, were pointing back to our eastern homes. Strangers, and in a strange land, memory had little need of being thus aroused, for although our faces were set westward, our hearts went quickly home, and our spirits heard the voices of those we loved, and we saw their familiar faces. . . .

The sinking sun, the deepening twilight, the gradual coming of the stars in their appointed order, and the stretching of the milky-way across the sky, will always affect one, even amid the dust and smoke of a city, but situated as we were, beyond the very borders of civilization, and almost beyond the abodes of men, the death of that calm, beautiful day, came like a sweet spell over the heart. Night came, clothed as it seemed, in her "festal garments:" she had put on all her stars. Above, the heavens glowed, and below, every blade of grass, and every little leaflet, sparkled also with its stardrop of dew. . . .

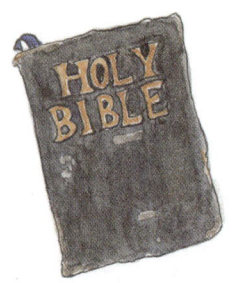

The Sabbath

Not long after arriving in the fall of 1854, the first citizens of Lawrence organized religious services as described by Reverend Richard Cordley in *Pioneer Days in Kansas.* Cordley immigrated to America in 1833 from Nottingham, England, with his parents, settling near Ann Arbor, Michigan. His father, a schoolmaster, made sure Richard received a good education, and eventually Richard went on to attend Michigan University and Andover Seminary. While attending Andover, Cordley and three friends formed the "Andover Band," a group who together pledged to go to Kansas upon graduation and make the Territory their "field of labor." The four arranged to go to Kansas employed by the American Home Missionary Society. The young Reverend Cordley arrived in the Territory in autumn 1857. Not long after, on December 2, he gave his first sermon at the Plymouth Congregational Church in Lawrence. His wife, Mary, came to Kansas in 1858.

Although construction began in 1857, the Plymouth church building remained unfinished until 1862, when the congregation dedicated the completed structure. Cordley served that church until 1875, and then again from 1884 until 1904. During Quantrill's raid in 1863, Cordley barely escaped death when guerrillas burned his home. In 1874, Reverend Cordley received a doctor of divinity degree from the University of Kansas. Later he served as a regent of the Kansas Agricultural College. Reverend Cordley died in 1904. In *Pioneer Days in Kansas,* Cordley wrote

about the first formal church service held in Lawrence, before he
had arrived, led by Reverend Samuel Lum:

*The first services were held in what was called the "Pioneer
Boarding House." This was a sort of hay tent. It was built by setting
up two rows of poles about twenty feet apart, the rows inkling
toward each other, and coming together at the top. The sides were
thatched with prairie hay. The ends were filled up with sod after
the manner of a sod house. The door was at the end, through the
wall of sod. This gave a room some fifty feet long and twenty feet
wide. The ends were all gable and the sides were all roof. This
served as the principal hotel of the town. On Sunday it was put
in order for religious services. Three trunks set one on the other
served as a pulpit, and the congregation seated themselves on the
beds and boxes and baggage of the boarders. There was always a
good congregation, as everybody attended church.*

*The forming of a church was one of the things talked of from
the first – even before the coming of Mr. Lum. They all wanted a
church–some because they loved the church, and some because a
church was the proper thing. . . .*

Lewis Litchfield, who arrived in September 1854, also wrote in his diary about the first service:

[A]s yet there had been no public worship in the new city there being no suitable place. But now Sunday had again arrived and the new boarding house being finished it was deemed best by all that there should be public religious worship forthwith. We had among us a very pious and devoted minister in the person of Rev Lumm, a native of the state of New Jersey who readily took charge of the divine services. Early in the morning of this holy day might be seen bodies of the pioneers busily engaged some washing at the pure spring of moving waters, and some arranging seats in the house for those who chose to come in. Very few seats could be afforded, and therefore these had new straw placed over the ground. At about nine o'clock all the camp assembled in the large house, together with some persons who had settled within 8 or 10 miles of us. How solemn was the scene. . . .

For settlers, the Sabbath was not only a day for worship, but also for reflection and enjoying friends' company. Robert Tovey wrote to his wife about the call of the church bell to the evening service, when he would deliver the sermon. Walter Hastings Woods reflected on a Sunday afternoon ride with friends. In her memoir, Melissa Genett Anderson described a trip to a camp outing, when she and her companions, though delayed by darkness, remained undaunted and arrived late for the gathering, but early for Sunday service. Chestina Bowker Allen remembered the kindness of the preacher's wife in a November 1856 diary entry:

Osawatomie, Kansas Territory
December 17, 1854

My Dear Wife
. . . Hope you are in good health now. I am glad to find that Eliza
gets on so well in her learning as to obtain the Medal. . . There is
one place of Worship here under the Chief Superintendent of the
Methodists although they do not object to other denominations
preaching sometimes. There is a cupola on the top with a Bell in it
to tell the people to come to church. My boss attends there regular.
But I must now wish you Robert & Eliza & all our friends a good
night as the Church Bell is ringing to tell the people to come & hear
me preach to night. I Remain your ever affectionate Husband,
Robert A. Tovey
 Robert Tovey
 From a letter to his wife

Sumner, Kansas Territory
Sunday, September 12, [1858]
It is a lovely day. I went to church in the forenoon, Brown,
Pearson, I, Emma, Mary, and Esther went out to ride in the
afternoon.
 Walter Hastings Woods
 From his diary

Allen County, Kansas Territory
In the fall of '59 the little school house began to make its
appearance. Also the itinerant preacher was seen oftener. Where
there were school houses, meetings were held in them. Where there
were none, services were held in homes.

Whenever there was the privilege of church, everyone for miles
around would yoke up the oxen and go. We often went three

miles for night meeting, and would find ox teams, standing all around the school house. In October, 1860, there was a camp meeting on Spring Creek, about three miles away. We planned to go Saturday and stay till Monday. A neighbor and his wife were going with us, and for some reason they did not get over till after dark. We started anyway, hoping that we would get there before the evening services were over. The road went straight for one mile, then wound around quite a large pond, and then went straight in the same direction. All four of us were riding in the wagon. Presently we heard the oxen splashing in the water, apparently having decided to go through the pond instead of around it. The men had to get out and start them again. It was very dark and we had no kind of light. We went on till we thought we were surely about at the camp. Then the oxen stopped. The men got out again, and found that the oxen were standing in front of the bars at the entrance to our own barnyard. But we were not to be disappointed, so we turned around and made the second start. We got into the camp just as the people were retiring, but we were ready for the Sunday services.

Melissa Genett Anderson
From The Story of a Kansas Pioneer

*Rock Creek, Pottawatomie County, Kansas Territory
Nov. 26th 1856
Rev. Blood preached and dined. Mrs. Blood sent me a present of two linen handkerchiefs, paper of hooks and eyes, spool of cotton, cord and two hairpins. . . .*

Chestina Bowker Allen
From her diary

Celebrations

In a proclamation made on November 27, 1855, James H. Lane, chairman of the Executive Committee of Kansas Territory, set December 25 as a day of thanks, though it was not officially recognized by then governor Shannon. Lane, a driving force in the Kansas Territory, received much credit for Kansas entering the Union as a free state. The Thanksgiving document from 1855 read:

> *In pursuance of a long established usage, which has always found a cheerful acquiescence in the hearts of a grateful people, and by the direction of the Executive Committee of Kansas Territory, I do hereby appoint and set apart Tuesday, the 25th day of December next, to be observed by the people of Kansas as a day of public Thanksgiving and praise. . . .*
>
> *Let the occasion be improved by the people of Kansas, for the advancement of Freedom, Virtue and Christianity – let the poor be remembered and relieved, and the day be wholly spent as Wisdom shall direct, and God approve and bless.*

In November 1856, settlers in the Territory enjoyed a peaceful atmosphere following a difficult and violent period of political unrest. Governor John Geary declared November 20 as a day of Thanksgiving. Considered the first official proclamation of its kind issued in Kansas, the statement came while Geary visited the Pottawatomie reservation near Topeka. Settlers Edward Fitch, John Ingalls, and Cyrus Holliday observed that holiday and other Thanksgivings in the Territory. Though they celebrated with friends and family, they remembered loved ones far away, as shown in their letters.

Lawrence, K. T.
November 21, 1856

Dear Brother,
I rec'd a day or two since a letter from you dated Nov. 6 and in it two dolls. which you say nothing about so I suppose the letter must have been opened and the bills put in . . . We had Thanksgiving yesterday in accordance with Gov. Geary's proclamation. The Ladies here got up a drive and the tickets were two dollars so that bill just bought my ticket. The proceeds are to be used to give a dinner to the Free State prisoners at Lecompton but I acted as door keeper and gave them a part of the time and so did not have to pay anything. . . .
. . . I am going to keep Thanksgiving next week at Mr. Savages where I stay at present. We shall have a kind of family party and I shall think of home much, especially if we have it on the same day you do in Mass. . . .
    Edward Fitch
    From a letter to his brother

Lawrence, Kan.
Dec. 23, 1857

Dear Parents
. . . I had a very good time as for the first Thanksgiving spent at my own home. . . .
I had Father W, George & Muzzy here to dinner Thanksgiving. We had baked beef and potatoes to eat. . . .
    Edward Fitch
    From a letter to his parents

Sumner, K. T.
21st, 11 mo. 1858

Dear Father
. . . I do not forget that Thursday next, is the anniversary of
our Thanksgiving, the first in which we as a family have been
permanently separated. In thought I shall join the familiar circle and
unite in the wonted festivities, remembering that though absence
and distance may separate, they cannot divide: they interpose no
obstacle to the passage of a happy memory and a fervent prayer. . . .
    With regards to all at home, Very Truly,
    Your Son,
    J. J. I.
    John J. Ingalls
    From a letter to his father

City of Lawrence
Kansas Territory
Dec. 3, [18]54

My Dear Mary –
This Sunday Evening I avail myself of the generous offer of a friend
to pen you again a very few lines – You will see by this that I have
got no place to call my home – But I hope ere long to have you with
me and then I feel that I will truly have a home. . . .
    I do wish you were here, Mary . . . I have found the very best
of people in Kansas. I am becoming more and more pleased
with them every day, and I know you would like them and the
place were you here – Last Thursday I was invited and attended
a "thanksgiving dinner" – Several gentlemen and Ladies were
pleasant – and we had a good time generally. . . .
    Holliday
    Cyrus K. Holliday
    From a letter to his wife, Mary

In 1860, just after becoming pastor of the Congregational Church in Topeka, Reverend Peter McVicar gave what he called the "First Thanksgiving Sermon." Reverend McVicar had emigrated to the Territory in October of that year after completing his studies at Andover Seminary. He enlisted and served in the Civil War. A proponent of education, Reverend McVicar later served as superintendent of public instruction in Kansas. In 1871, he took the job of president of Washburn University, where he served for twenty-five years. In his Thanksgiving sermon, Reverend McVicar mentioned the political climate of the Territory within the context of being thankful and hopeful for freedom and God's goodness:

Topeka, Kansas Territory
November 9, 1860
No.8, Hymn 34, "Ye nations round the Earth rejoice!"

We meet to-day on this western frontier of our land, to observe a religious & long established custom. A custom handed down to us from our earliest history as a people – Nor do we meet alone, our brethren of other states are met with us. At the same hour their songs of praise are mingling with ours, & their prayers have been already offered in our behalf. . . .
. . . This day however calls us together not only as individuals and families – but also as citizens of Kansas, as members of our adopted territory. Many of you came here in troublous times– many came from the peace & quietness of Eastern New England homes, to establish here those principles of freedom & religious liberty – which have been & are today the glory our land –
Dark and threatening were the clouds that hung over the early settlers of this Territory. The question was not one of individual or personal interest. It was a question between liberty & slavery – Here Freedom & oppression grappled hand to hand – The struggle was severe. . . .

*. . . We then as citizens of Kansas, have reason to make
this, especially, a day of Thanksgiving, in view of what has
been wrought out for us in the past, & in view of what we may
reasonably hope for in the future – We can not but feel that we
have entered upon a new & a brighter epock. . . .*

Autumn brought other reasons to celebrate. For Thomas Wells,
it was his marriage to Eleanor (Ella) Benes in 1856; for Axalla Hoole,
his birthday that same year; and for Peter Bryant, the election of
Abraham Lincoln in 1860.

Manhattan, K. T.
Nov. 2d, 1856
Mrs. T. P. Wells

My dear Mother,
I did not write home last week for I had enough else to occupy
my time.
The past week has been an eventful one to me, on Thursday
evening last (Oct. 30th) Ella and I were married. Everything
passed off pleasantly; 'twas a beautiful day, not a cloud to
be seen, and all guests that were invited came, except two,
and they were quite unwell; sixteen, besides ourselves and the
family in whose house we were married, were present, and that
is doing pretty well for Kansas, for you must know that they all
had to come from one to five miles over the prairies in the dark
and several of them got lost and wandered about for half an
hour or more before they could find the house. . . .

Douglas, K. T.
Oct. the 12th 1856

My Dear Sister
This is my birthday, and I must celebrate it by writing you a short
letter to let you know how I am on such a memorable occasion. . . .
Betsie is making me some apple dumplings in honor of the day. . . .
> *A. J. Hoole*
> *From a letter to his sister*

   Surely Peter Bryant's family must have looked forward to his letters from Kansas, with their colorful descriptions and lively language. In 1859, Bryant took his thirst for adventure and skill for writing west to the Territory, where both flourished. He settled in Holton, about forty miles north of Topeka, where he lived until 1862, when he returned to Princeton, Illinois. He married Henrietta (Kitt) Bacon, and in August enlisted in Company K of the Ninety-Third Regiment, Illinois Voluntary Infantry. The unit fought at Vicksburg, Mississippi. Bryant became very ill and at some point returned to Illinois to recuperate, remaining there until just after the Civil War ended in 1865, when he, his wife, and son, William, returned to Holton. After living a productive life as a farmer and community leader, Bryant died in 1912. In the following letter, Bryant shared his elation over the election of Abraham Lincoln as president:

Holton, Jackson County, K. T.
November 11th, 1860

Dear Brother
I have just received your letter of the 21st ult. First and foremost,
I congratulate you on the election of "Honest Old Abe." It makes
me feel good all over. 'Tis true I've been expecting it for some time,
but when I heard the news . . . I just "hollered" loud as I could
put in for two hours and a half, away out here by myself on the

prairie with nobody but "Deacon" and "Bully" to hear me, and I have not got over it yet. The fit comes on occasionally, and I yell out Hurrah for Old Abe! In a way that makes the heavens ring, and the echo from the hills on either side catches it up and sends back, Hurrah for Old Abe! Old Abe! Abe! All nature rejoices. The sun shines clearer and warmer, and I actually believe on this occasion the grass will sprout. Evening before last the northern lights gave a grand display, and last night during the shower, lightning played strange antics across the sky, and old thunder bellowed Hurrah for Abe!

Entertainment

In early Kansas communities, music provided a common bond that brought people together. The town of Lawrence enjoyed tunes from the Lawrence Band on many occasions. For Joseph Savage, one member of the band, musical entertainment often took place in his own cabin.

Our cabin that fall was the "head center" of music in Lawrence, and every pleasant evening we had concerts within and large audiences without. Our songs consisted mostly of Sabbath school songs and sacred hymns; frequently the crowd on the outside joined in, and often, at this day, do I hear men speak in grateful remembrance of our cheerful music in the rough cabin of 1854. . . .

    Joseph Savage
    From Recollections of 1854

Born in Connecticut in 1817, Lewis S. Bacon lived in Lawrence. He and Ellen Moor married on August 24, 1859, the ceremony conducted by Reverend Richard Cordley. His 1857 diary, written in sepia ink, included details about social events:

Lawrence, Kansas Territory
Sept. 10, 1857

A concert took place this evening, a kind of promenade concert all seemed to pass off well . . . Yesterday attended the Indian first fruits dance. All passed off well.
  Lewis S. Bacon
  From his diary

Lawrence, Kansas Territory
Herald of Freedom
September 19, 1857
The Promenade Concert, by the Lawrence Cornet Band, a week ago, was a very creditable affair, and reflected great honor upon the performers. All the pieces save one were loudly cheered, and some of them were encored. We were glad to observe that the concert was well attended, and all parties seemed delighted with the proceedings and music. We trust this Band will be induced to give another entertainment at an early day.

Members of the Delaware Indian tribe often came to Lawrence. Lewis Bacon recounted a day when part of the tribe danced in town. The *Herald of Freedom* mentioned the event as well, describing it as a "pow-wow." The article reported that accompaniment for the dancing came from an improvised drum, made from a piece of deerskin drawn over a nail keg. Bacon made several entries in his diary about visiting the Delaware. Chief Pachalkey of the Delaware Tribe, whom Bacon refers to, had also spoken at the first Fourth of July celebration held in Lawrence in 1855.

Sept. 14, 1857
This day the Delaware came into
town and danced to the great
amusement of the people. Pachalkey
made a speech. $10 were given them.

Nov. 9, 1857
Also a visit at Pachalkies, took supper
there in company with two soldiers,
after their arrival had a visit with
Pachalkey and wife. Distributed
candy among the children all passed
off well . . .

Originally from New Gloucester, Maine, Hannah Anderson married William Ropes at the age of twenty-five and settled in Waltham, Massachusetts. Several years later, Hannah's husband deserted her and their four children. In 1855, Hannah's eighteen-year-old son headed for Kansas Territory. Hannah, who held strong antislavery views, and her daughter, Alice, joined him later. Writing letters home to her mother in Massachusetts, Hannah eloquently, though not always favorably, described her life in Kansas. Many of her letters recounted her time spent caring for others. This caregiving capacity would manifest itself again a few years later as Hannah cared for wounded soldiers. In 1856, as the pro-slavery / free-state conflict grew more intense, Hannah returned to Massachusetts.

Strong in her convictions, Hannah began to develop politically and creatively, publishing two books, *Six Months in Kansas,* in 1856, and *Cranston House,* in 1859.

Influenced by Florence Nightingale and her elevation of nursing to a profession, Hannah volunteered as a Union Army nurse in 1862, and soon became head matron of the Union Hotel Hospital in Georgetown, an area of Washington, D.C. During her time at the hospital, Hannah worked successfully for better care and conditions, sometimes meeting strong resistance from doctors and the military. Louisa May Alcott worked alongside Hannah in 1862 and 1863, until Hannah's death from typhoid pneumonia in 1863. Alcott contracted the same illness but survived after a long recovery, gaining literary fame for her book, *Little Women*, written in 1868.

In an October 1855 letter to her mother, Hannah described the Lawrence military festival that she attended at the not yet completed Free State Hotel:

Lawrence, Kansas Territory
Oct. 20th [1855]

The dinner, given by the Kansas Rifles No. 1, was the result of
a hunting contest. Now "Uncle Jeff" comes to me with tea, and
the promise of a place by the fire tomorrow should the weather
moderate. He tells me, too, of a grand hunt which is to come off
in a week, the game is to be served up in the dining-room of the
yet-unfinished hotel. He presents me an invitation to the supper,
and is quite sure we shall all be well enough to attend. The week
rolls round: the game hunt is very successful; birds, turkeys, ducks,
squirrels, rabbits, and blackbirds, almost without number, are
brought in to the committee of superintendence. The tables are
well laid, and decorated with fancy cooking, got up under the
skillful supervision of a lady from Worcester. A pie made entirely of
blackbirds is an object of general interest. Whether there were the
proper nursery number, of "four-and-twenty blackbirds baked in
one pie," I am not able to learn. But the Party was very successful,
and most satisfactory to a larger number of people than ever
before met for amusement in this territory-many of the guests
coming thirty-five miles. . . .

    Hannah Anderson Ropes
    From Six Months in Kansas

Sara Robinson attended the same party and later recorded her thoughts about the evening:

Lawrence, Kansas Territory
Nov. 15th [1855]

Rainy and very chilly. A military supper in the evening. For two or three days men have been out in the woods hunting game; and to-night a large number of our citizens have gathered to partake of the supper, and join in the general festivities of the hour. Notwithstanding the rain, the mud being over shoes in depth, at an early hour the large dining-hall of the hotel was full of people, our neighbors and friends, while many came from miles away. A piano stood at the upper end of the room, parlor and dining-hall being thrown in one, and over the arch of the folding doors waved the "star-spangled banner," presented to the military companies on the fourth of July. . . . It was a New England gathering, though some, by their dress, tinsel ornaments, or their peculiarity of speech, showed that their home was further west. Some of the latter were asking continually, "When will the supper be ready? If there is going to be anything to eat, let us have it now." That our people are eminently social, the frequent public gatherings here and at Topeka will bear witness. A person coming in to mingle in the scene would never realize he was in a newly settled country, or in a town scarcely a year old.

Sara Robinson
From Kansas: Its Interior and Exterior Life

In Fort Scott, C. W. Goodlander and friends did what they could to improve the social scene by starting a dancing school and practicing Shakespeare.

Along about November 1, 1860, there were two traveling musicians came along, one by the name of Signor Forillo and the other by the name of George Peabody, – Forillo was a fiddler and Peabody a banjoist. After they had played several times for the boys, we concluded to hire them by the month to give concerts for our amusement, so we made a bargain with them for $100 a month, and after the first month we let Peabody go, but as Forillo claimed to be a dancing master, we hired him till spring to run a dancing school, and there is where all the early inhabitants of Fort Scott, both old and young, learned all they knew about dancing.

    C. W. Goodlander

    From Memoirs and Recollections of C. W. Goodlander of the Early Days of Fort Scott

L. A. McCord was a small wiry man and was cracked or had wheels in his head on the subject of the stage and was continually spouting Shakespeare. So as to show himself off he got a lot of us boys to consent to rehearse the act of Othello in the old hospital ward room, organized the boys and gave them their parts, reserving Othello to himself as star. Well, all McCord's theatrical company amounted to was several rehearsals with him doing the most of it, and he never did get far enough with his company to give an entertainment. . . .

    C. W. Goodlander

    From Memoirs and Recollections of C. W. Goodlander of the Early Days of Fort Scott

In 1859, Daniel Mulford Valentine, accompanied by his wife Martha, moved his law practice from Fontanelle, Iowa, to Leavenworth, Kansas Territory. He had spent the previous few years teaching and studying the law. After practicing law in Leavenworth for a year, Valentine then moved his practice to Franklin County, an area he later represented in the Kansas legislature. In his diary,

Valentine mentioned daily activities related to his law practice and social events he attended. He described the political atmosphere in Leavenworth in the days before the Wyandotte Constitutional Convention:

Leavenworth, Kansas Territory
FRIDAY, September 30, 1859
At Home – Beautiful day – Went at night
& heard the Hon. Anson B. Burlingame
make a Speech at Stocktons hall – he
was eloquent. a Speech consists more
in the Language used & the manner of
using it than anything else. he told very
little that was new to me yet but few
men could have told it so eloquently –
he is so eloquent but not fluent he often
had to pause for words. But when the
words came they were beautiful – he
was like Goodfellow he used eloquent
passages such as found in the Poets &
Poetic Speeches.

MONDAY, October 3, 1859
At Home – fine warm day – Heard Marcus J Parrott & S. W.
Johnston speak at night at corner [of] Shawnee and 2nd St. about
1500 2000 persons out –

THURSDAY, October 6, 1859
At Home – Cool but very fine day . . . Politicians on the corners
electioneering. . . .

Valentine managed to dodge the speechmakers to get to the theater, probably at Stockton Hall, built in late 1858. A few days later he attended a Masons meeting. The King Solomon's Lodge in Leavenworth was chartered on October 15, 1858.

FRIDAY, October 7, 1859
At Home – Pleasant day – warm – went to the Theater at night Play of the French Spy . . .

FRIDAY, October 21, 1859
At home – a very fine day – not doing much . . . Attended King Solomons Lodge No. 10 for the first time that I attended a lodge of Masons at Leavenworth.

TUESDAY, November 29, 1859
At Home – Very fine day a most beautiful day – bought Some flour &c. Went to hear Mr. A. D. Richardson Read a Lecture on "Out West." He is nothing uncommon. The Lecture was in the conversational Style. It was in the main a true picture of Western life and of the causes that induce men to emigrate to the West . . . .

Emporia, Linn County
The Kanzas News
September 10, 1857
                    Lecture on Kansas
Rev. Daniel Foster will deliver a lecture on "Kanzas and her Pioneers," in the hall under the Printing Office in Emporia, on tomorrow, (Sabbath) at 10-1/2 o'clock, A. M. The intimate acquaintance of the lecturer with the past history of Kanzas – her struggles and trials – eminently fit him to handle this subject, and we expect a rich treat on the occasion.

Though Kansas pioneers left much behind when they set out for their new home, their interest in knowledge and culture came west with them, as shown by the social organizations they formed.

A literary society was organized in Topeka as early as the fall of 1855, under the name of "The Kansas Philomathic Institute" . . . Its purpose was for self-improvement, by contribution of literary compositions, public readings, music, the accumulation of a library, and dramatic study. . . .

From Thirty Years in Topeka by F. W. Giles

Hesper, Kansas Territory

But with all our hardships and misfortunes, we did not forget the intellectual side of life. It was in 1859 that our nearest neighborhood, 4 miles east of us, began to agitate the idea of a literary society. A meeting was held and a committee appointed to solicit membership. One day in October I was surprised to see a white woman coming on horseback over the hills. She finally stopped at my door, and after talking with Mr. Sears and his cousin about the proposed literary society she rode up to my door and introduced herself as Mrs. Eliza Conger and invited me to be a member of the new society. You may be sure I was not long in saying: "Yes, I shall be pleased to become a charter member and to know there is some place where I can enjoy the social and intellectual side of life. . . ."

I never regretted that I became a charter member of the Hesper Lyceum. This was one of the joys that came to me in the West. Even though the road was long and dreary and we were sometimes weary, our faithful team, "Buck" and "Broad," always carried us safely there and back with our precious load of little ones; for we always took our children along with us, with comforts and buffalo robes to keep them warm. I derived much benefit from the association I formed at this society, for they gave me new courage to bear up and go bravely on. . . .

Mary A. Sears

From Pioneering in Kansas

Personal Pursuits

As the weather turned colder, Joseph Trego and others spent time in their cabins reading and writing letters. As Joseph Trego so tenderly put into words, letters to and from loved ones brought comfort to a lonely heart. Settlers would walk miles, sometimes more than once a day, hoping to find news from home in familiar handwriting. Some settlers played chess, read books, or even made furniture. Samuel Reader viewed the night sky with friends and kept up with world events, including the Siege of Sebastopol (1854–55) that occurred during the Crimean War.

Our log cabin at Sugar Mound
Oct. 16th [1857]

My Dear Wife,
I did not think I would have deferred writing you so long as this. It has been three weeks, and a few days over perhaps, since I wrote you from Kansas City, the day of our departure from that place. I will say, right here, that I will write as often as I want you to, in future, and that will be once every week. . . .
. . .Have received but one letter from you yet but suppose another is close at hand. I will be much disappointed if I don't get one this week yet. We have three mails per week.
We have an abundance of the best kind of water mellons. When travelling between here and river could hook plenty of

*fine ones by the road, in the state. I am getting cold too and wood is
scarce in the cabin as we have to carry from the grove all we burn,
having no team yet, but I feel as tho I could write all night it seems
so much like talking to you, for I have been writing now a long time,
with your likeness on the paper and every time I stop to dip my pen
in the ink I see your sweet face; how glad I am that I have it, guess the
case will be pretty well worn for I carry it all the time. . . .*

    Joseph Trego
    From a letter to his wife, Alice

Lawrence, Sept. 19, [18]55

Dear Father,
*. . . I have dated this letter Lawrence but am writing it in my log
cabin on my claim . . .*

    *Why under the sun don't the boys or some of the rest write to
me? I want to know about the farm–whether you have any apples
& Peaches, are you making any cider? And lots of things . . .*

    Yours as ever
    E. P. Fitch
    Don't forget to answer immediately.

Lawrence, Sept. 30 [1855]

Dear Parents,
*If the adage is true that what we have but little
of we prise highly, it must be that "Letters from
Home" are very valuable with me for I have but
few of them . . .*

    *I have got my house done and am now writing
in it. I let the lower part . . . and keep the upper part
to sleep in myself. I have got all my things here–a chair,
table & book case and I can sit here and write or read at my ease . . . .*

. . . It has been very cold here for a few days so that on low lands there has been some frost but not much, not so much but we are still haying around here.

Yours as ever

Edward P. Fitch

Sumner, Kansas Territory

Monday, 3d October 1859

It is a lovely day. We all staid at home to day. I am reading Chilty's General Practice.

Walter Hastings Woods

From his diary

Near Sugar Mound, Kansas Territory

October 22 Th. Dull & rainy – After getting thro' with the morning work I began on a new chair which I design keeping as a memento of the present pioneer life in this country. It is made of hickory saplings with the bark on. Intend giving it a coat of varnish to keep worms from getting under the bark . . .

October 25 S. Used up the day in reading, writing, picturing &c

Joseph Trego

From his diary

Indianola, Kansas Territory

Friday, [October] 5, 1855

Heard that Sevastopol has fallen. 70,000 killed on both sides. 70,000 Russ. Prisoners. Mr. Holliday of Topeka was here today. Left us a Topeka paper.

Sunday, [October] 7, 1855

Got pawpaws, Read Bonaparte.

Monday, [November] 23, 1857
Fixed an end to my spyglass and a screw to pistol . . . Kate Wallace
and others a soiree du chant . . .

Sunday, [November] 29, 1857
Rainy. 35 degrees. Cold. Read Mohicans in French. A bad day.
Wrote my Journal up to date.
    Samuel J. Reader
    From his diary

Leavenworth, Kansas Territory
SUNDAY, October 30, 1859
At home – cool day – Reading - & thinking about writing an
address on liberty –

FRIDAY, November 11, 1859
At home – Rather Pleasant but cloudy morning turned cold very
Suddenly about 3 O'Clock & a very cold evening – Went to Dr.
Obriens & played Chess –

FRIDAY, November 18, 1859
At Home – cool & cloudy . . .
Bought Chequer Board &
Men 85 cts –

SUNDAY, November 20, 1859
At home all day – cloudy day Sometimes it rained a little – Read
– Poetry &c –
 Daniel Mulford Valentine
 From his diary

Council City, Kansas Territory
THUR., 20 September 1855
Warm & south breeze. Took a good bathe in the morning, went to Hoovers, thence to Alisons, took dinner there, thence to Brattons, thence to Prentises, got half bushel corn meal, thence home, read Paines Age of Reason.

SUN., 23 September 1855
Warm, scattered Clouds, a few drops of rain. Lay back reading, wrote 4 letters.

SUN., 5 October 1855
Cloudy & cool. Felt better, went out and cut some corn, went down to the Post-office in the evening, received 8 letters and a bundle of papers, Came home & read my letters & papers.

TUES., 23 October 1855
Very cold & windy. Sat by the fire all day & read.

THUR., 25 October 1855
A little cool, rather windy. Husked corn greater part of the day. Read philosophy some.
 James Stewart
 From his diary

Thoughts on Kansas

Eureka, Kansas Territory
Oct. 27, 1857
Found all well and prosperous. Surveyors came on to survey the
town site surveyed a part of it only, felt quite buoyant in regard
to the future prospects of our town in hopes to have a sawmill in
a short time Black-smith Shop etc moved into our house about
Nov. 6 felt remarkably well never any healthier. There is a kind of
excitement to life in a new country a per-son is brought into scenes
with which he is not familiar, there is constantly something new
and novel, there is pleasure felt in starting new, in opening a farm
where before nothing but the Deer & the Antelope have roamed
over the prairie free as the air they breathe. . . . Here where the
Wolf's howl has pealed forth upon the still night air unheard by
human ears, where the grass has sprung up in living green – the lap
of generous nature – where ten thousand flowers have blossomed
but to "waste their sweetness on the desert air" where the trees
natures temples have been vocal with the thanksgiving songs of
the birds whose notes were heard only by the ear of Him who gave
them life, here I fain would make my home would plow & fence
& build & see the work of my own hands make what was once a
lonely waste a thrifty home. . . .
   Edwin Tucker
   From his diary

Winter

Rock Creek, Pottawatomie, Kansas Territory
Jan. 1st, 1857

A new year has commenced. How solemn
the thought the wheels of time have so rapidly
brought us hither. Let us be thankful that we
are yet an unbroken circle since our soujourn
in Kansas, with health improving and prospects brightening. We will ever trust in and
praise the Great Ruler of all things.
                              Chestina Bowker Allen

Winter ushered in a time of both ending and beginning, a sense
of completion and renewal. As the year came to a close, men and
women reflected on the extremes that life had presented in the
past months—the excitement of finishing a cabin, the sorrow of
losing a friend, the camaraderie of neighbors, the yearning for
one's family. For some, winter was a time to weigh sacrifices and
accomplishments, a time to decide whether or not to stay come
spring. John and Sarah Everett, of Osawatomie, had been through

one cycle of seasons and felt encouraged, as John wrote to his parents in January 1857:

The prospect before us this summer is brighter than it has been yet in Kansas. Our health is much better. The look for peace and confidence is yet good. The prospects of an overwhelming preponderance of free state settlers here are not at all desperate but highly encouraging. I hear on all sides noise of anticipated improvements the coming season. . . .

Improvements did come to the Everetts' town of Osawatomie and to other emerging towns throughout the territory, as shops and businesses opened to serve the growing communities. In Lawrence, businessman James Blood advertised a selection of goods including boots and shoes, clothing, crockery and glassware, hardware, and plaster. In the January 24, 1857, notice, published in the *Herald Tribune,* Blood called special attention to his grocery department, where molasses, candles, and more filled the shelves of his new store. After procuring supplies from Blood's, a shopper could stop at Wilmarth's Books and Stationery for reading material, or to peruse their selection of wallpaper for something to brighten up the cabin.

Few people arrived in the Territory during the winter. Local officials and merchants looked ahead in anticipation of the spring rush, although some industrious souls could not wait. Just in time for Christmas, the *Kansas Tribune* of December 23, 1858, carried an ad for a new "Candy Manufactory," in Topeka, that touted "fancy and other qualities of superior candy" made on the premises. A bakery connected to the candy store had cakes, pies, fruits, and nuts, and could furnish said items for weddings, balls, and parties. Optimistic about the enterprise's future, the owner announced that an ice cream "saloon" would open in May. Just as one year ended, settlers excitedly looked forward to the beginning of the next.

In Sugar Mound, Joseph Trego looked forward to building a future for himself and the town, where he owned a sawmill. Trego helped to develop the community, including initiating plans for new roads. In a letter to his wife, Alice, still in Illinois, Trego wrote that keeping busy helped take his mind off his loneliness and the sometimes-gloomy weather. John Ingalls mentioned the "moist melancholy weather," in a December 1858 letter to his father, but added, "and yet the fine days are so beautiful as to compensate for a larger amount of ambiguous weather." When snow came, the situation went beyond moist and melancholy, as John Deering found during a nighttime storm in February 1858. While he and his cabin mates slept, the swirling blizzard winds blew the cabin door open, sending drifts of snow inside. One of the "bachelors" jumped up and got the door closed, but the morning found the beds covered with snow and the men experiencing "a cold time generally."

When weather permitted, settlers happily joined their neighbors at church, a party, or a lecture. In 1859, presidential candidate Abraham Lincoln traveled through the Territory, but local newspapers reported little about the Illinois senator's visit to Kansas in late November and early December, possibly because it fell between two overshadowing events—the Lincoln–Douglas debates the previous year, and the upcoming 1860 presidential election. Lincoln did not have the support of Kansas Republicans. That support belonged to the more-popular Republican vying for the party's nomination, William H. Seward. Lincoln vehemently opposed slavery and condemned the violence between free-state and pro-slavery forces in the Territory that had made news across the country. Lincoln repeated his antislavery views in each town along the way, beginning with Elwood on November 30.

From there he made stops in Troy, Doniphan, and Atchison. In Leavenworth, the last of the five Kansas stops, Daniel Mulford Valentine heard Mr. Lincoln speak against the Territorial policy of popular sovereignty. Lincoln left Kansas on December 6. At the Republican Party's convention in 1860, candidate Lincoln received the nomination and went on to win the presidency. The flag that flew at Lincoln's inauguration on February 22, 1861, had thirty-four stars, the newest representing Kansas, the state whose history had captured the nation's attention at a crucial time in its own.

In 1856, Lawrence residents, including Hannah Ropes, paid tribute to another president, George Washington, on his birthday, at a ball hosted by the Kansas Rifles No. One, the first military company organized in Kansas. Charles Puffer attended a ball in Lawrence in 1858 that also honored Washington. Earlier in the winter, settlers had celebrated Christmas and New Year's. From the 1858 New Year's Hop in Osawatomie to the small turkey dinner with James Mead in Salina in 1860, diaries, letters, and newspapers provided colorful details of the holidays.

Although winter presented additional challenges, moments of celebration warmed the hearts and buoyed the spirits of growing communities. Isaac Goodnow, esteemed citizen of Manhattan, experienced just such a happy time on January 17, 1856, when he turned forty-two years old. He wrote in his diary just how he spent the day: "Got me a cat! Treat of pie & cake. . . ." Heartened by small pleasures, settlers looked ahead to the promise of spring.

Emigration

Though emigration almost came to a halt during the winter months, this did not preclude people from thinking about it and planning for spring, when wagons would once again be rolling across the greening prairies and growing towns. Although excited about the prospect of more citizens, the *Herald of Freedom* warned emigrants to bring with them adequate supplies and abundant spunk:

Herald of Freedom
January 13, 1855

A Crowd in the Spring

The eastern emigration to this Territory in the spring will be immense. We have letters from all parts of the country seeking information, and telling of companies which are forming to locate in this Territory. All right! Come on; but prepare for pioneer life, else you will get disheartened, and wish yourself in the East again. The man who comes here self-reliant will do well, and the more of that class the better, but those who wish to fall back upon Emigrant Aid Companies, or on private individuals for support, had better remain away; for they will only return with reports of broken promises, disappointed hopes, ruined constitutions, and, worse than all, - empty purses.

Lawrence, Kansas Territory
Herald of Freedom
January 13, 1855

Topeka

A new town site with the above name has been selected, and is now rapidly filling up with eastern people. It is located about twenty-five miles above this point, on the Kansas River, and will probably be a point of considerable importance. Several of our most active business men are connected with the movement, and they are bound to make it "go-ahead." It is said there is a fine country around it, and that nature has been prolific in her bounties. A steam saw mill, and all the various appliances of civilization will be introduced there upon the first renewal of navigation in the

spring. The name is said to be the original Indian one for the Kansas River. A friend who resides in the vicinity, promises to give a description of the place, and keep us fully advised of transpiring events.

In 1857, John Bayless from Kirkwood, New York, arrived in Kansas, and with four other men formed the Highland Town Company. He joined his daughter, Cemantha Minion, and her husband Abram, a merchant, already living in the area. Located in the northeastern corner of the Territory, the town of Highland soon began to take shape. Bayless built a hotel in the new town later that same year. In January 1856, while still living in New York, Mr. Bayless wrote a letter of encouragement to Cemantha, and told her of his plans to move to Highland:

Kirkwood, Broome County, New York
January 14, 1856

Dear Daughter,
Your kind letter of the 2nd Dec (although we saw it was mailed
some days after) came to hand this morning. We were very
glad to hear from you, and that you liked the country. I know
you have many Privations in Kansas, but I think you will have
no reasons to "regret" having done something toward settling
that fine Country. There is nothing either great or good that we
can accomplish without an effort. This winter will be the most
trying time for you and Abe. But <u>Courage and Perseverance</u> will
overcome all obstacles. I certainly can see but very little object
in any one staying here. And I intend to sell & move out as
soon as I can. I think I can do it in the Spring. Whether I sell or
not I shall if my life & health is spared come to Highland in the
Spring. . . .
The children all send their love to you all. Write often.
From Your Father who loves you
John Bayless

Once settlers arrived and began to construct homes, they
often had to be creative in the selection and use of building
materials. It took some time to get sawmills established. When
milled lumber became available, not everyone could afford it.
Tradespeople such as carpenters and plasterers began to arrive
early on in Lawrence, Leavenworth, and Topeka, but their services were expensive. For some settlers, constructing a house or
suitable shelter before winter set in meant using whatever they
could find and afford. An article from the Lawrence *Herald of
Freedom* described one interesting and versatile building material. Cyrus Holliday also explained the use of other natural sub-
stances, in a letter to wife Mary:

Lawrence, Kansas Territory
Herald of Freedom
January 13, 1855
Cotton Cloth
From the immense quantities of the above article sold in this place, it is very evident it has entered into use in other forms than that practiced in the eastern States. We are told that some persons have been known to buy as many as ten pieces at a time for their own consumption. The curious reader who will take the trouble to look in upon our pioneer residences will soon discover where the cotton muslin goes to which is brought into Kansas. In the first place it is used for roofing; some giving the cloth a coat of tar, with a sprinkling of lime. It is very generally used for lining up rooms in the inside, and, if papered afterwards, makes a warm and comfortable ceiling, and would very likely be mistaken for a plastered wall. It has been, until quite recently, used mostly for doors. The eastern reader wonders at the necessity of a resort to such expedients for finishing up rooms; but if he was acquainted with the difficulty of getting material for plastered walls, of course his surprise would cease. . . .

Lawrence, Kansas Territory
December 3, 1854
The gentleman who favors me with the priveleage of writing this note says if you will come out he will immediately surrender all right and title to his mansion – It is one of the best in the place – I will describe it – In shape it is exactly like the roof of an ordinary house – about 14 ft long – the floor is Earth – such as the Creator made – next the frame work of the building – which are rough poles stuck together – it is a layer of brush – next a layer of sod or turf – and next a covering of prary grass – If you like the accommodations, let me know. . . .
   Cyrus K. Holliday

Though winter weather hindered travel, one could still imagine the journey. Territorial newspapers frequently ran original verse, such as "Let's All Go to Kansas," that painted an enchanted picture of the region.

Herald of Freedom
January 27, 1855

Let Us All Go to Kansas

Let us go to the West, and there build a cot,
To those far distant wilds, to some beautiful spot,
To the plains of fair Kansas, where the bright waters flow,
To the land of bright promise, dear wife, let us go.

Let us go to sweet Kansas, and find there a home,
Where turmoil, and strife, and contention ne'er come,
Let us find a green slope where the soft zephyrs blow,
To that garden of beauty, dear wife, let us go.

Let us ALL go to Kansas, that Eden-like land,
Where the flowers spring in beauty and the breezes are bland,
Let us plant there a garden and dress it with flowers,
And spend our few days amid its green bowers.

Then we'll sit there at eve and watch the wild roe,
As bounding in freedom o'er the prairie they go;
We'll drink in the music that melodious floats
O'er the flower-decked prairie, in tintinabulous notes.

We'll listen enraptured to the whippoorwill's lay
As it steals on our ears at the close of the day;
We'll gaze on the wildwood, on nature at rest,
And sing of thy beauty, oh! Glorious West!

To the home of our childhood we'll bid a good-bye,
We'll take a sad look, and from it will hie,
We'll gaze on the graves where our kindred repose,
Oh! Saddest of all are our parting with those.

The Natural World

Robert Gaston Elliott came to Lawrence from Indiana in 1854 to publish a newspaper, the *Kansas Free State*, with his partner, Josiah Miller. The two met while attending Miami University of Indiana. In May 1856, after one year of operation, the paper was destroyed during the attack on Lawrence by pro-slavery advocates. The paper went to press again in 1857 in the town of Delaware, near Leavenworth, but published only two issues. Elliott went on to serve in the Territorial legislature from 1857 to 1858. In November 1860, following the long drought, he served as secretary of the relief convention held in Lawrence. Elliott continued to serve in public office on the state board of agriculture and as Douglas County treasurer. He died in 1917 in Lawrence. In a letter to his sister, Mary Jane, in 1858, he described the weather and discussed plants for her new home:

Lawrence, Feb. 20, 1858

Dear Sister,
. . . .The weather has been delightful this
winter. I have never seen a more
pleasant season – Yesterday and
today have been as balmy as Spring.
For about two weeks we had cold but
calm weather, just enough to furnish a
good supply of ice – which has been stored
in abundance for summer use. . . .
    I suppose you have got into your new
house. . . . Now that spring is coming you must
not neglect to set out trees and shrubbery and
have the garden arranged. You know my taste
about Elm trees and Maples. Don't forget them.
Osage Orange makes a pretty shade tree and is of
quick growth. I saved last fall the seeds of several varieties
of our wild flowers which I will send if I have not lost them.
    Enclosed you will find a few seeds of the Prairie Rose. It
grows to the height of one or two feet and has a very delicate
and beautiful flower. The Persimmon seeds were grown on the
town site of Delaware and have been carried in my pocket for the
last three months. I might have saved a large variety of very fine
flower seeds, but when the seeds are ripe it is almost impossible to
distinguish them. . . .
    Yours truly,
    R. G. Elliott

Winter seemed a good time to think about spring, seeds, and
gardens. James Griffing wrote to Augusta Goodrich about plans for
planting, and requested that she bring some seeds with her on her
trip to Kansas:

Wakarusa, Kansas Territory
Saturday, Dec. 2, 1854

My Dearest Augusta,
. . . . When will you be ready to come and live in a little log cabin?
Only set the time when most suitable and I will endeavor to
be ready—if you can consent to sacrifice so much. Next June or
September will be the most favorable times for me as I wish to spend
all my spare time in trying to improve my claim. Could you have
collected choice cherry, peach, plum, or pear seeds, garden seeds of
any kind, they will all come very acceptable. I have engaged some
fruit trees and want to do as much as possible the first year. I hope to
get several acres improved. . . . Please write when convenient. Give
all the news. Remember me to all inquiring. And ever believe you will
share the sincere wishes of your best friend,
    James

As pioneers moved west, they encountered a variety of animals, many they had not seen, or heard, before. Originally from Woodstock, Connecticut, Moses C. Sessions settled in Linn County in October 1857, where he lived until his death in 1868. He shared his observations with acquaintances through vivid descriptions. In this letter from January 1858, Sessions lists the wildlife on the "perary," including the noisy wolves:

Centerville, Linn County, Kansas Territory
Jan. 10, 1858

Dear Sir
I take my pen this morning to let you know that we are yet a live
and where we aree left Union the 17th of Sept 1857 and arrived at
Centervill Lin Co on the 17th of October where we now are. . . . there
is plenty of Timber perhaps from one to two miles wide and verry

*good it consists of black wornut Oak of all kinds maple hackbury
Sigamore Elm &c. . . . tell Frank & Milo that thair is plenty of deer
wild turkeys perary hens wild gees here the gees cum in to our corn
fields they lite on the perary near the house by hundreds woolvs are
verry plenty they cum round the house Some nights and make Such
a yelling that it wakes us all up I got up one night and went out in my
Shirt and drove them a way &c. . . .*

    Respectfully yours,
    Moses C. Sessions

Even the mice staked their claims in the Territory, and, thanks
to the settlers, had shelter from the winter cold. Hannah Ropes
took a whimsical approach to the creatures that shared the space
at her hotel. She documented the scene in a letter to her mother.

*Lawrence, Kansas Territory
February 1856*

*There is no space of this room which they have not measured with
their rapid feet; and no secret hiding place they have not peered into.
Harmless always, except in taking a bite of everything eatable, they
make themselves perfectly at home. If the room is still, they amuse
me by their frolics upon the floor; and often they play "possum,"
by rolling themselves up and dropping from the stone wall down
to the floor below. Often, in the night, they make a short cut across
the bed's head, spring thence to the books, scrambling among the*

papers, for a night's entertainment. Woe be to any delicacy, if they get at it! We learn at home to say, "still as mice," but that saying grew out of ignorance of this miniature race of creatures. One should be deaf, to sleep well where they are. Such dissipated night merry- makings as they have can hardly be recorded of any other race; and their grace of motion is beautiful indeed.

    Hannah Ropes
    From Six Months in Kansas

In January 1855, both James Griffing and the editor of the Lawrence newspaper noticed local birds. Griffing gave a detailed description of them in his letter to Augusta:

Lawrence, Kansas Territory
Kansas Tribune
January 13, 1855
Tuesday last was one of the most lovely days
we ever witnessed in January. The bluebird
has made its appearance, and are seen in
flocks, denoting the approach of spring. . . .

Wakarusa [Kansas Territory]
January 18, 1855

My dear Augusta,
. . . . I ought to have excepted the birds which flock about my cabin in great numbers since the snow. They seem very glad to get a few crumbs of cold Johnny cake which I scatter out to them. The chickadees and snowbirds are most numerous. There are a few birds here [that are] the most beautiful and which have staid about most of the winter. The principal one is the paracheet, of most beautiful green with a yellow head–nearly as large as a dove. Quite a flock of them came the other day and stopped near where

I was. Two of their number remained as sentinels in a tree whilst the remainder flew down to the shore of a stream and sought food. But my favorite bird here is about the size of a robin with a little horn on his head nearly an inch in length. He is of a beautiful light red color and is a prince in song. The thrush can't begin to sing with him. Such is his variety [of songs] that you would almost think he had a dozen music pipes at his command. If I only had about a dozen of them about in my cabin, others might go to Trinity to hear music but let me remain among my birds and hear it from nature's perfect voice–where I may listen to loftier and smoother cadences and sweeter and gentler tones. . . .

Adieu for the present. The Lord bless you and keep you is the prayer of your,

James
James Griffing

Entertainment

Chickadees and cardinals could fly all year, but for Kansas settlers, winter weather sometimes called for a unique mode of transportation. Sleighs on the prairie might be a bit less fashionable than those in the East, but still provided riders with an enjoyable time.

Topeka, Kansas Territory
Kansas Tribune
March 10, 1859

Sleighing

I've a proud, prancing steed; like the wind for speed –
And the downiest robes of the West,
And the gayest of sleighs for the winter days –
The season that I love best;

And, I've something beside to give zest to the ride,
Something better and brighter than these;
I've a dear little maid, who is never afraid
To be kissed by the cold and the breeze.

Let it blow, let it storm, there are bosoms as warm
As if winter had never been known,
For 'tis little we care for the wintry air,
And the snow 'round the hill tops blown;

We've a soft fur fold for each breath of the cold,
And we nestle like birds in a nest;
Ho! Hurrah, for the boys and the sleigh-riding joys
With the maidens whom they love best.

J. M. Fletcher
Written for the Kansas Tribune

Topeka, Kansas Territory
Kansas Tribune
December 16, 1858
Sleighing seems to have been the only source of amusement for a
few days past. We noticed four horses hitched to a sled proceeding
up the Avenue, going at the rate of 2:40, on yesterday. The only
bells that we use–cow bells–were suspended to the horses necks, in

*numbers to make the music complete by creating a fanciful discord
and away they went with a merry laugh – not the horses that
laughed, but the inmates of the sled- Ladies and Gentlemen.*

At the age of thirteen, George O. Wilmarth moved to Kansas
with his father, Otis; his mother, Julia; and his half-sister, Sarah.
Shortly after the family's arrival in Kansas, they befriended Edward
Fitch, who later married Sarah. In the winter of 1856, Otis opened
the first bookstore in Lawrence and subsequently opened another
store in Topeka. An 1868 Topeka city directory listed the book and
stationery store, and showed George as living in Topeka. In an 1858
letter to a cousin, George describes the design and construction of
a prairie sleigh:

Lawrence, K. T.
Wednesday Eve., March 24, 1858

Dear Cousin Sophia
*. . . . We have been having most delightful weather this winter
and but a very little snow and no sleighing except for about two
hours one morning the sleighs began to run a little but before
noon the sun came out warm and carried the snow all off so you
can guess how much there was of it. I wish you could see some of*

our Kansas sleighs if they wouldn't make you laugh. I will try and describe one to you. They are made with two long limber poles with a notch cut about half way in each so that they can be easily bent without breaking, one end of each serve as runner and the other as fills. Then there are two upright sticks in each pole (at the end which is meant for the runner) with a wide board across the top which serves as seat so now you know how a sleigh looks. This kind of concern is all that they can afford in this country for we don't have sleighing enough to use what sleighs we already have. Oh wouldn't it be fun if one of them should be drawn through the streets of Boston. . . .

George Wilmarth
In a letter to a cousin in Braintree, Massachusetts

Lawrence, Kansas Territory
Thursday, [February] 10, 1859
This evening I was up to the lodge. No work today. Today it snowing very hard. . . .

Friday, [February] 11, 1859
Very good sleighing to-day the weather is very pleasant.
Orvis Hubbell
From his diary

Sumner, Kansas Territory
Thursday, December 9, 1858
It is a fine day. River froze over to-day. We moved the Engine down part way on sled in forenoon. Ox sick to-day. Colburn worked on doors in P M. Jim & I teamed timber. Wheeler came back. I got a letter from Father. About 8 in. of snow & good sleding.
Walter Woods
From his diary

After a busy day of sleighing, singing, and dancing, Anna Margaret Randolph shared a sweet fantasy with the trusted pages of her diary:

Emporia, Kansas Territory
December 6, 1858
A sleigh ride and singing school on this day. Met with better success than any other sleigh ride – didn't break down or meet with any accident. Had a good time singing and some dancing. Their cabin was something like the cabins we read about in novels –the pretty rag carpets, papered walls, white curtains, and –oh! What luxury that big rocking chair must be. I think I could live very contented in such a house with my only male. We could draw our armchairs around the little stove and talk. It would be honeymoon all the time. I would always have things bright and cheerful, and he would be so good and wise, and I would be so proud of him. There! My candle is out. I'll have to get to bed.
 Anna Margaret Randolph

Other winter activities kept the settlers indoors. In December 1859, Abraham Lincoln's train pulled into Elwood, Kansas, the first of five towns he visited on his pre-election trip to the Territory. Perhaps the best account of this visit came from Leavenworth attorney Daniel Mumford Valentine, who attended Mr. Lincoln's two Leavenworth speeches and provided interesting descriptions of Mr. Lincoln's mannerisms and appearance:

Leavenworth, Kansas Territory
SATURDAY, December 3, 1859
At home forenoon Reading afternoon went down in Town Jenny Cole & another promenading the Streets Went to the Lincoln's Reception at Mansion House He is an Old man Tall Slim and awkward and farmer looking. Col. Vaughan made reception Speech and Lincoln Replyed in a few remarks. There were quite a number out perhaps 500 - Went at night to hear Hon Abe Lincoln make a Speech. Stocktons Hall was crammed full, all parties out, the old man spoke 2 hours. It was a Sound deep & logical speech he is not eloquent like Burlingame, - his language is not so beautiful, his periods not so nicely turned his questions not so graceful, his hands were placed one on the other & both at his belly at the commencement towards the conclusion he kept them on his groins or upper part of his thighs one on each thigh the most of the time, he occasionally made gestures with his hands, he is not Poetical, he States everything fairly. His forte is (after stating his opponents views and arguments fairly & justly) to reduce those views and arguments to a palpable absurdity & to show them in a ridiculous & Ludicrous light, The Points he touched on were ably handled as

*I have ever heard or seen them handled. I think it as able a speech
as I ever heard.*

MONDAY, December 5, 1859
*Went to Hear Hon. Abe Lincoln make another Speech – he has the
actions of a Kentuckian he aims to Say Something funny but he
does not try to use beautiful Language, he got off several good hits,
his Language is his own & Original – Do all Kentucky orators try to
Say Something funny? . . . .*
    Daniel Mulford Valentine
    From his diary

Kansas settlers brought many cultural traditions with them.
The literary society was one activity of intellectual culture that
became popular early in the development of prairie towns. In
Topeka during the winter of 1855–56, the Philomathic Literary
Society, also known as the Kansas Philomathic Institute, held its
first meetings. The group gathered each Saturday evening in Union
Hall for discussion and literary readings, with the first Saturday of
the month set aside for lectures. In 1857, the Society began produc-
ing a handwritten "journal" called the *Prairie Star,* which featured
the poetry and prose of its members. In the inaugural issue, dated
January 24, 1857, the editor, Maria Martin, opened with reflections
on settlers' perspectives as they huddled inside for the winter:

*With the early days of the bright New Year, while the cold
Searching winds come Sweeping o'er these broad Prairies, entering
every creek and crevice of our Kansas Homes.*
    *We circle round our quiet firesides, each busy with his or her
own thoughts, thankful for the measure of peace which now is
ours after the distracting Scenes of the past year–*
    *The man of business as he rests from his daily toil, thinks of his
prospects, how much he may make by his last speculation. What*

the receipts of his last years labors were. How he will provide and act, for the future. The Mother thinks of the home She has left, of the valuable Schools, the many advantages which formerly surrounded her youthful family and earnest hopes that the Same may ere long Surround her and hers, in this there far Western Home. The young wife with busy thoughts intent, building up in her imagination her little home with all of Nature and Arts adornments . . . but bright dreams for the future occupy her every thought. And the young man, and blooming maiden full of gaity and mirth, and bright anticipations, Transplant to there new homes, Some of the Scenes and enjoyments of former homes. First, and most valued among we consider our "Literary Society" . . .

In January 1857, the Institute celebrated its first anniversary, highlighted in the *Kansas Tribune*. According to Cutler's *History of Kansas,* the gathering included speeches and readings by L. C. Wilmarth, L. Farnsworth, and Mr. Joseph C. Miller, a tinsmith and hardware store owner.

Topeka, Kansas Territory
Kansas Tribune
January 5, 1857
The anniversary of the Philomathic Institute took place at Union Hall last Saturday evening. It was a fine affair, and reflects much credit, enterprise and ability of our citizens.

Kansas Tribune
February 2, 1857
A poem will be delivered by Mr. Loring Farnsworth, before the Philomathic Institute at its next regular meeting, on Saturday evening the 7th inst. The interest in these exercises is rapidly increasing, and their merit well repays the attention they receive.

Kansas Tribune
February 15, 1857
An interesting feature in the weekly
entertainment of the Philomatic
Institute, is the "History of Topeka,"
which is published in fragments
in the paper which the ladies read
before the Institute each week, and
which is of itself, a very interesting
and attractive part of the exercises.
Meetings on Saturday evenings, at
Union Hall.

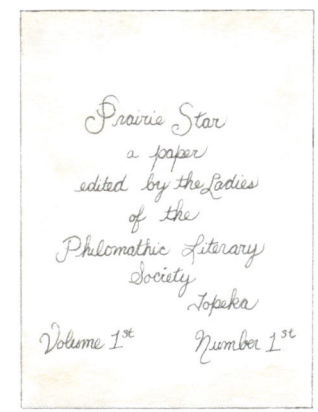

Kansas Tribune
February 10, 1859

Philomathic Institute

The regular weekly meetings of this Institution are becoming
more and more interesting. The meeting of Saturday evening last
was largely attended, and a good deal of interest manifested by
the members present. The best and most pleasing feature of these
meetings, is the reading of the paper. Miss Carrie Whiting, one of
the editors, prepared the paper last week, which was particularly
interesting. Members of the Institute should take pride in lending
a hand to the editors, in contributions, as these papers will be
looked upon, in years that are in the future, by those who are
called upon to perpetuate an institution framed in the early
history of Kansas.

In Lawrence, the Athenaeum provided similar opportunities
for intellectual stimulation with a variety of topics and speakers.
The group also established a library.

Lawrence, Kansas Territory
Herald of Freedom
January 13, 1855
Kansas Athenaeum
J. B. Emery, Esq., of this city, gave a very interesting discourse in Eloquence and Oratory, before the Kansas Athenaeum, at St. Nicholas Hall, on Tuesday evening, to a full house. We were not able to be present, but learn it was highly satisfactory. The next address of the season will be delivered at the same place a week from next Tuesday evening, by S. C. Pomeroy, Esq.

Herald of Freedom
January 24, 1855
Athenaeum
The question for discussion on Tuesday evening, the 30th inst., is as follows:
Should the policy of non-intervention on the part of our government be departed from in the present contest in Europe?
  Aff. J. Hutchinson, J. Mailey
  Neg. J. Speer, E. Clark

Herald of Freedom
January 27, 1855
Books for the Athenaeum
Several books have been received from Mrs. Amos A. Lawrence, whose husband, the town's namesake, and Mrs. Mary Webb of Boston, for the Lawrence Athenaeum, and a large addition to those already received will be sent on to this city in the spring, when navigation opens.

Our Athenaeum, though young and in its infancy, starts with fair prospects of becoming one of the first Literary Institutions in the country. May it prosper, and shed its benign influences over the minds of all the inhabitants of Kansas, is no doubt the ardent wish of its pioneer founders.

For less-intellectual indoor winter activities, Walter Woods and Orvis Hubbell sang, danced, and went to the Lodge. In Lawrence, the local sewing groups hosted a grand party that included a supper and a speech by James Lane, and Melissa Genett Anderson wrote about a prairie-style surprise party, where the hosts were the ones surprised.

Sumner, Kansas Territory
Friday, December 10 [1858]
I got a paper from Henry. It is a beautiful day. We finished moving the Engine down today with 3 yoke of oxen. Colburn & Charley fixed sled in afternoon. Parker mills drawed timber. Mills works for 1.00 a day now. I went to a dance & sing at Sumner House in evening with Mary.

    Walter Woods
    From his diary

Lawrence, Kansas Territory
Tuesday, [February] 1, 1859
No work to day very pleasant weather this Evening I went to Singing School at Lawrence

Thursday, [February] 17, 1859
This forenoon I work but this afternoon I did not work Up to the Lodge as usual This evening I went to a surprise party at Miss Thompsons some great time

Friday, [February] 25, 1859
To work as usual in the shop the weather is very fine this evening went to a social hop at the Eldridge House a good time

    Orvis Hubbell
    From his diary

Lawrence, Kansas Territory
Herald of Freedom
January 9, 1858
*The several sewing societies in Lawrence gave a Union Festival at
the Johnson House on Tuesday evening last. There were nearly
two hundred persons in attendance. The supper served up by the
hostess of the Johnson House, was very excellent, and did credit
to the ladies engaged in preparing it. A war speech, made by Gen.
Lane, about nine o'clock in the evening, precipitated matters,
and broke up the social circle, which till then had been unusually
interesting.*

Emporia, Kansas Territory
*We had a pleasant winter. Everyone within five miles was our
neighbor. It was not at all strange to have a wagon load of people
drive up to stay all day, entirely without warning. People did not
wait to be invited. They would just come, and then fly in to help get
dinner. . . .*
    Melissa Genett Anderson
    From her diary

Celebrations

The many parties and balls gave local newspapers plenty to write
about over the Christmas and New Year holidays. The personal
writings of John Henry Deering and C. W. Goodlander show that
even in small towns in Kansas, pioneers knew how to have a good
time. William Goodnow and James Mead rang in the New Year
in a quieter way. On Christmas Day, Mead had a turkey dinner,

and Goodnow visited with "Brother Denison," probably Joseph Denison, on New Year's Day.

Topeka, Kansas Territory
Kansas Tribune
December 26, 1857
The Christmas party, at the Chase House, last evening, was a happy affair. The congregation of gallant beaux and "merrie maidens" was fair to behold. The supper-but we won't speak of that, we couldn't do it justice. It was just such a supper as Chase can get up. We left the party at a late hour, in the successful tide of huge enjoyment. May our young friends be permitted to see a good many more such, is our fervent wish.

Topeka, Kansas Territory
Kansas Tribune
January 1, 1859
Holiday Festivals
The Christmas Festival held in this place on the evening of the 24th inst., reflected honor on its managers. The whole thing went off in good style and to the entire satisfaction of all present. The Masonic Festival was well represented by members of the order, and likewise gave much credit to those interested in making the necessary arrangements for a grand good time, which those present enjoyed.

By December 1859, James Mead had settled on the Saline River, where he and two other men had established a business trading with local Native Americans. Writing to his mother one year later, Mead apparently had settled in Salina, where he made a profitable living, selling hides and meat. In the 1860 letter, Mead assured his mother that he would be having a good turkey dinner that Christmas day:

Salina, Ks.
Dec. 25, 1860

My dear Mother:
While you are roasting that big turkey for your Christmas dinner, I
will write you what I am about. It has been some time since I have
been down to get my mail and I found
6 or 8 letters waiting for me and ever so
many papers. We are going to have a
good dinner pretty soon, as I shot a fine
wild turkey this morning and Mrs. Jones,
who by the way is a model housekeeper,
is cooking it. . . .

In haste, your son
James R. Mead

Leavenworth, Kansas Territory
FRIDAY, December 23, 1859
At Home – At Dist Court – Cold morning & Snowy – fine but cool
evening – Quite a number of dances balls festivals banquets.
Soirees Suppers &c. and Gift enterprises Advertised for this &
next week.

Daniel Mulford Valentine
From his diary

JAN 57

Indianola, Kansas Territory
Thurs., [January] 1, 1857
Obscur. Le vent et Sud Froid [Cloudy. The wind is cold and from
the south] . . . P.M. Snowy.

Samuel J. Reader
From his diary

Topeka, Kansas Territory
Kansas Tribune
January 5, 1857
The New Year's ball, which came off at Union Hall, on New Year's
Eve, was a fine affair; a general good feeling seemed to prevail;
all seemed to enjoy themselves in the very best manner possible.
Those who attended will have pleasing recollections for a long time
to come, of the first New Year's Ball in Topeka.

Topeka, Kansas Territory
Kansas Tribune
December 16, 1858
              New Years at Brownville
We are informed that the people of Brownville are to have a
"Grand New Year's Festival" at Heath's Hall, on the evening of the
31st. inst- The best supper and the best music that the country
affords will be provided for the occasion.

Joseph N. Bourassa, a Pottawatomie Indian and an interpreter
for the Pottawatomie Agency, used his Indian name, Ke Kahn, to
sign this letter about arranging music for an upcoming ball. The
recipient of the letter, Thomas N. Stinson, worked as an Indian
trader with the Delaware and Pottawatomie. The Shawnee Indians
adopted Stinson and gave him the name Ne Kahn. In 1854, he
founded the town of Tecumseh, on the Kansas River east of Topeka.

C[ouncil] Grove, Kansas Territory
Dec. 29, [18]56
Mr. Thos. N. Stinson.

My friend.
Will please to inform the Gent. Committee that, with a considerable
difficulty I distributed their Tickets–they were sent to me, at too late a

day, to give out to advantage. The best dancers are nearly all invited to two or three Balls given on the same day. Notwithstanding that I have got ladies enough for about two sets-Lafromboise father and son, M Beaubien Darling and may be some others will go. I have got Albion Allcott, for first Violinist, and I have heard C Beaubien will go down for assistant player. We, (our folks) will try to go on Wednesday to your place. Tell Mr. Vaughan that I have done all I could for them–I will take down my Violin cello–to be out ten ta.

Yours in haste
Ke Kahn
Joseph N. B.

Lawrence, Kansas Territory
Herald of Freedom
January 6, 1855

New Year's Supper

In company with a large number of our citizens, we had the pleasure of partaking of a New Year's banquet, on the evening of the 1st inst., at the boardinghouse of Litchfield & Burleigh, of this city. We were disappointed, first, in seeing so many ladies in attendance, hardly supposing there were so many in the Territory; and secondly, in finding on the occasion so great a variety of dishes, and all so excellently prepared. We seemed to forget, for the time being, that we were away from the conveniences and refinements of eastern life. All appeared in excellent health and spirits, and, as one speaker very happily remarked, rather contrasted with the condition he was told in St. Louis he would find the people in–that the Yankees at Lawrence were literally starving for the necessities of life.

Mr. Litchfield was the pioneer in Kansas in the way of keeping a boardinghouse. We are informed that he commenced operations by a large log, in the open air, where he did his cooking, and has worked his way along, sometimes feeding as many as two hundred and fifty persons per day at his "pioneer boardinghouse." . . .

Palmyra, K. T.
Friday, January 1st, 1858
Arose at sunrise. Breakfast of corn cake bread, and sorghum
cold and windy went over to Bloods Store and wrote up diary for
last year. P.M. made arrangements to attend dance at Palmers.
There was a call from Colonel Abbot to go down to Olatha for the
purpose of protecting polls on Election day 4 Oclock started with
Doct Martin and Mr. Gill for Soules arrived at 6:30 from thence
walked across the Prarie a distance of two miles to Mr Palmers,
scarcely any of the company had arrived and we had sufficient
leisure to survey the premises an get the hang of the school house.
Commenced dancing at 8.30, and danced at intervals until 12
when supper was served which was done in A 1 style. Very cold
during the night Wakarusa was there, and hoed down in fine
style. Sarah Jane lost her shoe but it didn't make any difference
to either you or I. It was big pig little pig root hog or drink with
them and all went merry as a marriage bell. I made some very
fine acquaintance, and was well pleased with the arrangements.
Wakarusa left about 4 and we had another dance which lasted
until daylight went up on top of Mount Washington where we had
a delightful view of the surrounding country.

> *John Henry Deering*
> *From his diary*

Manhattan, Kansas Territory
Tuesday, January 1, 1856
Therm Sunrise -8 degrees M. 29. Sundown 14 degrees. A Happy
New Year! 2150 miles from my former home. One year ago! Visited
at Br Denison's . . .

> *William Goodnow*
> *From his diary*

In 1860 I built a residence for Alex. McDonald on a lot where the Union block now stands. This was the first residence built of any pretensions, outside of the government quarters and at that time was considered the palace of Fort Scott. Alex. Made this residence a welcome place for all his friends, and many lively times were had there within its walls. New Year's calls in those days was quite a fad, and what few families were here always kept open house. This house of Alex's is the one where a lot of us were calling on New Year's day, when a young tinner by trade, now a staid banker of Fort Scott, rode his horse up the steps and into dining room, took his drink from the hostess on horseback, rode around the table and out the same way he came in and did no damage to glassware or anything else. . . .

C. W. Goodlander

From Memoirs and Recollections of the Early Days of Fort Scott

Continuing her series of letters to the Concord, New Hampshire, *Independent Democrat,* Julia Louisa Lovejoy sent a warm New Year's greeting to the editor and readers. In this letter, she also acknowledged the aid and support given by citizens of her native New Hampshire:

Lawrence, K. T.
Jan. 4, 1857
Dear Democrat: Most heartily do we wish thee, and thy readers,
scattered o'er our dear native hills, a "happy new year." From this
far-off land, we greet thee with a thousand good wishes, for thy
future prosperity. Thy sympathy with the oppressed and suffering,
of this, our adopted home, excites our warmest gratitude. . . .
    Julia Louisa Lovejoy

Winter celebrations didn't end with New Year's Day. Settlers found time to celebrate two special days in February—Valentine's Day and George Washington's birthday.

Topeka, Kansas Territory
Kansas Tribune
February 2, 1857
Our young folks, will find
at J. Willits' a supply of very
nice Valentines. The first
that have found their way
as far west as Topeka.

Lawrence, Kansas Territory
Feb. 24, 1856
Dear Parents,
. . . . The Merchants of Lawrence had an oyster supper on the
14th inst, speeches etc. & closed with a dance. I was one of the
Merchant princes attended and had a good time. . . .
    Edward Fitch

Washington's Birth-Day Ball
BY THE
Kansas Rifles No. One
Yourself and Lady are respectfully solicited to
attend a Ball, to be given at the
Free State Hotel
In Lawrence, on
Friday Evening, February 22, 1856
In honor of the Day which gave birth to the
IMMORTAL WASHINGTON
Tickets $2.00

Lawrence, Kansas Territory
February 22, 1858
Made soap and went around town in the forenoon. Weather cool
& pleasant. in afternoon went up to Mt Oread and Fort Lane. Ball
in eve. Firing of cannon.
    Charles Puffer
    From his diary

Lawrence, Kansas Territory
Feb. 24, 1856
The Military Com or rather one of them, Com. A, gave a ball on
the 22nd, Washington's birthday, but it was stormy & they did not
have a very large gathering. . . .
    Edward Fitch
    In a letter to his parents

Lawrence, Kansas Territory
Feb. 22, 1856
This twenty-second of February witnesses a social gathering in
the hall of this hotel, or rather in the dining-room. "Company A"
gave the party, and preside over it with a great deal of hospitality.

Tables are spread in the upper entry, which is very spacious. I am quite surprised at the clean and nice appearance of the tables, and the variety spread upon them for our refreshment. In the course of the evening, "Company A" entertain us with an original song got up by them, in the ballad style, giving quite a history of this settlement. . . . The month of February closes full of hope and cheerfulness to us all. . . .

Hannah Anderson Ropes
From Six Months in Kansas

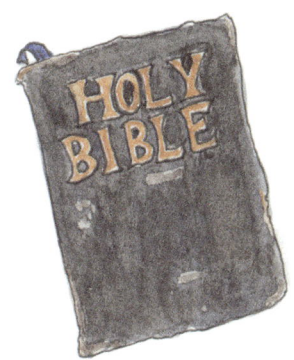

The Sabbath

Religion played an important role in the life of early Kansas. Ministers, including Reverend Charles Lovejoy and Reverend James Griffing, traveled with the first organized parties of emigrants. To settlers, organizing Sunday gatherings and providing education—Sunday school and public school—was high on the list of community priorities. The year 1856 presented Lawrence with the challenge of "the troubles," a term used to describe the violence between pro-slavery and antislavery factions. As pioneers often did, they found a solution that allowed them to carry on with daily life.

The first Sunday in January, 1855, a Sunday-school was regularly organized by Mr. S. N. Simpson, who was chosen the first superintendent of the first Sunday-school in Kansas. Some families had now arrived and there were a few children. The school met in a little building on Massachusetts Street, twelve by fourteen. . . . Twenty or thirty scholars met here every Sunday. Later on, as the troubles increased, it was not easy to maintain either Sunday school or Sabbath worship. During the following year the people were subject to constant alarms, and the school was not held regularly, but called together from Sabbath to Sabbath. If on Sabbath morning the danger was not too close, and military duty not too pressing, a bright boy would run round and notify the children that "there would be Sunday-school that day." The children were always ready, waiting for the call, and would come from all quarters. When the exercises were over they would disperse and wait for another call. They all became so accustomed to this state of things that any Sunday they could get the school together in an hour. The citizen soldiers would come in, hang up their rifles, and sit down to study the Word of God.

Richard Cordley
From Pioneer Days in Kansas

Lawrence, Kansas Territory
Herald of Freedom
January 13, 1855

Sabbath School

A Sabbath School was organized in this city on last Sabbath, under the auspices of Mr. Simpson, who has built an office on Main street, and generously thrown it open for the religious education of the children of this place on the Sabbath. He is entitled to the warmest thanks of the public for his labors in their behalf. Who is there who will be equally liberal in furnishing a house for a day school?

Herald of Freedom
January 20, 1855

Free Day School

We observe with very great pleasure that a subscription paper has
been passed around town with a view of raising funds to establish
a free school. A sufficient amount will be secured to keep the school
in operation for three months, after which, we presume, a like sum
will be raised. Mr. Edward P. Fitch opened a school on Tuesday last,
in the room in the rear of Dr. Robinson's office, with about a score of
students. It is presumed the number will be doubled in a few days.

Hesper, Kansas Territory
I should like to describe in more detail the social and community
life of these pioneer days. My husband built the first schoolhouse
after taking a public subscription to raise the necessary funds.
Here the community gathered for its literary, religious and social
activities. I recall that Mr. Sears was superintendent of the first
Sunday school in which I taught a class of young people. This
school was established by the Presbyterian Church. I think also
of the singing school, the first one of which Mr. Sears taught,
being a lover and student of music all his life. The lyceum was
a big event every week during the winter months, calling forth
the real intellectual forces of the neighborhood. The religious
revivals stirred the people
deeply, as they were usually
led by Free Methodists such
as the famous Lovejoy, who
stood flatly upon the tenets of
the old theology. . . .

> *Mary Sears*
> *From* Pioneering in
> Kansas, Iowa to Kansas
> in an Ox Wagon

Personal Pursuits

To avoid the worst of the winter weather, settlers spent time inside, visiting with friends, singing, or reading books and newspapers. For new citizens of the Territory and interested subscribers in the East, territorial newspapers provided a wide spectrum of information. At the *Herald of Freedom* office, settlers could obtain German as well as American newspapers. From their readers, the editors requested patience and emphasized that the news from Kansas would not come all in one issue:

Lawrence, Kansas Territory
Herald of Freedom
January 13, 1855

Be Patient

Some of our friends seemed to suppose that we were going to give a perfect description of everything in Kansas Territory in last week's issue of our paper, and were almost out of humor, we understand, because some things were overlooked. Be patient, friends. There are forty-nine more numbers due you to complete the first volume of our paper, and you will get one each week; and if you don't find what you desire this week, wait until next. Perhaps, by doing so, you will find all you desire. We must not give you all the news at once. Should we do so, future numbers would be comparatively worthless. Did you ever think of that idea before; sapient reader?

After a day spent building and repairing wagons in his shop, John Deering enjoyed singing, visiting with friends, and playing euchre, a game that involved trump suits, bidding, and taking tricks. He also spent time reading a variety of authors, including Charles Dickens and William Makepeace Thackeray. A serial novel that began in 1854, Thackeray's *The Newcomes* followed the romantic and economic exploits of English colonel Thomas Newcome and his son, Clive. At the end of the day, sleep brought visions of family.

Palmyra, K. T., Bachelors Retreat
Saturday, January 2, 1858
Eve Debating Society met at our cabin, and had a good time. . . .

Saturday, January 9, 1858
Down to Brooks and pitched in to Josephs wheels, had very bad
luck, broke gauge and v tool. Shot at Prairie chickens. P M worked
on wheels, fitted boxes in two of them, and rounded the others
home after smoked, and laid down dropped asleep, and slept until
10-30. Boys came home and we all retired. I was elected vice Pres
of Palmyra Eclectic club.

Tuesday, January 12, 1858
Up and baked bread Stayed in the house and played Euchre with
Charley. Down to Brooks went hunting, and treed one rabbit.
Home and had a Rabbit stew. P. M. walked over to Prairie City
with Brooks, very pleasant weather. Eve played Euchre some &c
Read Tribune.

Sunday, January 17, 1858
Barnes & Cutters Hotel Laid and talked with the boys about down
east and getting married. Stopped, and partook of their Bounty
and then pulled out for Palmyra at which place I arrived about
12. Very warm and pleasant to day. Found the Boys writing, went

in to Bodwells and got something to eat Down to Brooks, and had
a sing. Back to cabin and Sundayed up. Started for home. . . .
Arrived at Dumas about 4 After Tea conversed with Mr Gill about
Kansas wars and troubles until I was tired and sleepy Sought my
couch with a sense of relief and thankfulness. Dreamed of home
and of seeing Father was overjoyed to think he was alive Still knew
it was a dream Strange.

Palmyra, K. T.
Saturday, January 30, 1858
Down to Brooks and finished helve, carried C. C. saw down
and sawed up some hickory logs. Dinner P. M. Helped Brooks
haul wood. Very hard work this hauling wood. Presented with a
pumpkin pie by Mrs B home and prepared supper cooked pork
and mush, waited for the boys. They came at last, and brot some
milk and Doughnuts from Mrs Craigs A numerous congregation
to see me eat Played Euchre with Charley In Bloods and wrote
up diary for three days, Wrote to L P Fisher and went home, from
thence in to Bodwells, and danced until 12 Lucy Dora Delphine &
Hanson there had a live time.

Wednesday, February 3, 1858
Down to Brooks after getting breakfast, worked on hubs until 4
Oclock home dinner. Snows quite fast. Started at 5 for Prairie City
arrived at Caniffs about Sundown disappointed in our business
Supper at McAllisters. Spent the Eve at Giffords singing best time
since coming into K. T.

Sunday, February 7, 1858
Down to Brooks, and travelled round the woods ate supper Eve
read Dickens.

Sunday, February 14, 1858
Bitter cold and disagreeable Frenchman called for his wagon
and paid me $23. Read Thackerys Newcomes, hard keeping
warm . . .
    John Deering
    From his diary

Daniel Mulford Valentine kept busy in Leavenworth with his law practice and social events, but when at home, he enjoyed reading Robert Burns's poetry and Shakespeare, and playing a good game of chess. When Reverend Samuel Adair finally had some free time to read, he found some great news about Kansas in the local papers:

Leavenworth, Kansas Territory
THURSDAY, December 1, 1859
At Home all day – Very cold, a very Sudden change in the weather
last night – Reading Burns Poems –

FRIDAY, December 9 1859
At Home – Fine day – wrote letter to Sarah Valentine – At Mansion
House for dinner – played two games of chess –

WEDNESDAY, December 28 1859
At home – not cold but cloudy day. Money extremely Scarce . . .
Reading Shakespeare –
Daniel Mulford Valentine
From his diary

Osawatomie, Kansas Territory
Jan. 4 [1861]
Monday – recd – 2 sacks Wheat, 2 of corn, & 1 of beans, per Benj
Bell, probably sent by my old friend Jesse Dickenson – Read in the
papers to day that Kansas is admitted into the Union – now a State.
Samuel Adair
From his diary

For Cyrus Holliday and Robert Elliott, the cold winter brought time for warm thoughts of home and reading and writing letters to loved ones. No fancy writing desk was needed, as Cyrus Holliday showed:

Lawrence, Kansas Territory
January 7, 1855
I am now writing this sitting on a trunk and writing upon the end
board of a wagon which I am holding in my lap. . . .
Your loving husband HOLLIDAY

Lawrence, Kansas Territory
February 11, 1855

My Dear Wife-
As you will see by my heading I
am again in Lawrence and have
just begged a sheet of paper from

a friend to write you my usual quantum of Sunday talk. I should
be at church at this time instead of writing, but I had to walk some

four miles from the Country where I was stopping last night with Mr. Waterman–a friend to Mr. Ingram and myself–and I got in too late for service. . . .

I have had no letter from you since I wrote you last – nor I think since I wrote you two letters. This perhaps is not attributable to you so much as to the mails. I understand today that the mails between Chicago and St. Louis have been blocked by snow and ice for some ten days or more. Hence I expect when a mail does come I will receive a whole package from you. I hope so indeed. . . .

Your loving husband
C. K. Holliday

Lawrence, Kansas Territory
Feb. 15th 1858

Dear Sister,
I have now written quite a number of letters to the folks at home and about home and have received only two for 3 or 4 months. But I must not complain, but write, and write again. I suppose the rule is when any body leaves home, to write back every few days, and let his friends know all about himself – but if he wants to hear from them he can gather up his duds, travel back and go round and see them. . . .

Talking about riches – if hopes and anxieties, disappointments, and troubles were marketable, I would have been rich long ago – and might now have a princely fortune. I manage to get along however without letting what is called trouble and misfortune vex me, believing that:

Gnarling Sorrow hath less power to bite
The man that mocks at it and makes it light. . . .

Yours truly,
R. G. Elliott

Thoughts on Kansas

Lawrence, Kansas Territory
Feb. 24th 1856

The ice in our river dissolves its winter-union to-day—this twenty-fourth day of February—a bright, cheerful Sabbath. The sky appears in its own peculiar clearness, bringing distant objects distinctly before the eyes. I go from one window of the hotel to another, uttering exclamations at the prospect. I see the river curving quite round, up towards its source, walled with tall, tastefully arranged trees, and, floating sluggishly upon its surface, cakes of ice thick enough to have done justice to a more northern latitude. Groups of people stand along the shore, watching with apparent interest the indications of a clear and navigable river. While, from many little homes, church going people pick their way through the softened snow, pools of dirty water, and mud of uncertain depth, towards the rude place of worship. Off in the distance, towards the south-west, Blue Mound lifts its fair proportions against the sky, making a line with the Wakarusa river, marking its course by the fringe of trees along its nearest banks; and its farther shore, by the rising, terraced slopes lifting themselves far in the distance to the line of the horizon, sprinkled here and there with patches of clean snow, upon a ground of dried grass and the black mould of this truly fertile country. Without any great stretch of the imagination, one can fancy many distant towns and villages nestled in those pleasant slopes. One can never look over this beautiful country without a feeling of astonishment that it was never taken up for settlement before.

The month of February closes full of hope and cheerfulness to us all. The winter is indeed gone, and our places of abode are still standing unmolested.

Hannah Ropes

From Six Months in Kansas

In the January 24, 1857, issue of the Philomathic Institute's *Prairie Star*, the author, "Gusty," captured the spirit of hope that led intrepid pioneers through the difficult and sometimes turbulent times of early Kansas:

Hope

"Hope is the Anchor of the Soul," if it were not for hope, Says one, the heart would break. When we look forward with bounding expectation to some happy event Oh! How the heart expands, how Joyous we become, how happy we are; we are all life and animation. The world looks beautiful indeed, in our eyes all Nature Seems to Smile, and we cannot see why others do not

partake of our joyfulness. But truly we are creatures of an hour, let a change come, let us be disappointed in our expectations, how the heart sinks; how desponding; all Nature Seems changed, everything wears a gloomy aspect, even the birds Seem less gay in there Song, every thing wears a melancholy tinge. But let one ray of hope down upon us, What a revolution; again we see the sparkling eye, bounding expectation, and joyous heart. Hope points to the relmns of Eternal day, where there is continual sunshine and Storms never come. . . .

APPENDIX A: THE WRITERS

Name	Emigrated From	Arrived in Territory	Settled In
Adair, Samuel	Ohio	November 1854	Osawatomie
Allen, Chestina Bowker	Roxbury, Massachusetts	Autumn 1854	Rock Creek, Pottawatomie Co.
Anderson, Melissa Genett	Randolph County, Indiana	November 1857	Coffey Co., Woodson Co.
Bacon, L. S.	Connecticut	1854 or 1855	Lawrence
Bayless, John	Kirkwood, New York	Spring 1857	Highland, Doniphan Co.
Bourassa, Joseph N. (Ke Kahn)	Native American		Tecumseh area
Boynton, C. B.	Traveled through Territory	in 1854	
Brown, John Stillman	Massachusetts	1857	Lawrence
Bryant, Peter	Illinois (?)	Spring 1859	Holton, Jackson Co.
Carruth, Jane	New York	June 1856	Osawatomie
Carruth, Lucy	New York	June 1856	Osawatomie
Colt, Miriam	New York	May 1856	Neosho River, 30 miles west of Fort Scott
Cordley, Richard	Michigan	November 1857	Lawrence
Deering, John Henry	Bath, Maine	1856	Palmyra, near Baldwin City
Denison, Henry	?	?	Manhattan
Elliott, Robert Gaston	Cottage Grove, Indiana	Autumn 1854	Lawrence
Everett, Sarah	Oneida Co., New York	Spring 1855	Lawrence
Edward Fitch	Massachusetts	October 1854	Lawrence
Gilbert, Robert S.	Suffolk County, England	Autumn 1855	Douglas Co.
Giles, F. W.	New Hampshire	Autumn 1854	Topeka
Goodlander, Charles W.	Milton, Pennsylvania	May 1858	Fort Scott
Goodnow, Isaac and Ellen	Providence, Rhode Island	Spring/Summer 1855	Manhattan
Goodnow, William	Norway, Maine	Spring/Summer 1855	Manhattan
Griffing, James	Indianapolis, Indiana	November 1854	Tecumseh, Manhattan
Hildt, George	Canal Dover, Ohio	June 1857	Southern Johnson Co.
Holliday, Cyrus	Meadville, Pennsylvania	Autumn 1854	Topeka
Hoole, A. J.	Darlington, South Carolina	April 1856	Douglas Co.
Hubbell, Willard Orvis	Hornellsville, New York	?	Lawrence
Ingalls, John J.	Massachusetts	October 1858	Atchison

Name	Emigrated From	Arrived in Territory	Settled In
Learnard, Oscar E.	Vermont	Spring 1856	Lawrence
Lines, Charles B.	New Haven, Connecticut	April 1856	Wabaunsee
Litchfield, Timothy Lewis	Cambridge, Massachusetts	September 1854	Lawrence
Lovejoy, Julia Louisa	New Hampshire	March 1855	Manhattan, Palmyra, Leavenworth
Mayo, Elisha Frank	Massachusetts	April 1855	Lawrence
Mayo, Thankful Sophia	Massachusetts	September 1855	Lawrence
McVicar, Mayo, Thankful Sophia	Eastport, Massachusetts	October 1860 September 1855	Topeka Lawrence
McVicar, Peter	Eastport, Maine	October 1860	Topeka
Mead, James R.	Iowa (?)	?	Salina
Miller, Joseph C.	Rhode Island	March 1855	Topeka
Minion, Mrs. C. J. (Cemantha)	Kirkwood, New York	1855	Near Highland, Doniphan Co.
Puffer, Charles	Wisconsin	1858	Burlington
Randolph, Anna Margaret	Ohio	September 1858	Emporia
Reader, Samuel J.	La Harpe, Illinois	May 1855	Indianola
Robinson, Sara T. L.	Fitchburg, Massachusetts	May 1855	Lawrence
Ropes, Hannah Anderson	Waltham, Massachusetts	September 1855	Lawrence
Savage, Joseph	Hartford, Vermont	October 1854	Lawrence
Sears, Mrs. Charles (Mary)	Iowa	July 1859	Hesper, Lawrence
Sessions, Moses C.	Connecticut	?	Centerville, Linn Co.
Stewart, James R.	New Castle, Pennsylvania	November 1854	Council City (Burlingame)
Stinson, Thomas N.	Ohio	1854 (earlier as Indian trader)	Tecumseh
Tomlinson, William	Traveled through Territory	in 1858	
Tovey, Robert Atkins	Albany, New York	October 1854	Osawatomie
Trego, Joseph H.	Rock Island, Illinois	March 1858	Sugar Mound (Mound City)
Tucker, Edwin	Beloit, Wisconsin	May 1857	Eureka
Valentine, Daniel Mulford	Fontanelle, Iowa	July 1859	Leavenworth
Walter, George	Traveled through Territory	in 1855	
Wells, Thomas	Rhode Island	March 1855	Manhattan
Whitney, E. S.	Massachusetts (?)	1856	Lawrence
Wilmarth, George	Providence, Rhode Island	November 1855	Lawrence, Topeka
Wilmarth, Otis	Providence, Rhode Island	November 1855	Lawrence, Topeka
Woods, Walter Hastings	Massachusetts	1858	Sumner

APPENDIX B: WILDFLOWERS AND WOODY PLANTS FROM SETTLERS' WRITINGS

Writer's Reference	Common Name (possible)	Scientific Name	Writer	Location
WILDFLOWERS				
Golden Coreopsis	Golden Coreopsis	*Coreopsis grandiflora* Hogg ex Sweet	Sarah Everett	Osawatomie area
Indian Paint	Fringed Puccoon	*Lithospermum incisum* Lehm.	Sarah Everett	Osawatomie area
Japan Lily	Michigan-lily	*Lilium michiganense* Farw.	Miriam Colt	Neosho R., Allen Co.
Lamb-tongue / adder tongue w/white flowers	Field Pussy-Toes	*Antennaria neglecta* Greene	Sarah Everett	Osawatomie area
Larkspur	Prairie Violet	*Viola pedatifida* G. Don	Miriam Colt	Neosho R., Allen Co.
Plant with pods containing liquid	Milk-vetch	*Astragalus crassicarpus* Nutt.	Sarah Everett	Osawatomie area
Plum	Ground-plum	*Astragalus crassicarpus* Nutt.	Thomas Wells	Manhattan
Portulaca	Kiss-Me-Quick	*Portulaca pilosa* L.	Miriam Colt	Neosho R., Allen Co.
Prairie Rose	Prairie Rose	*Rosa arkansana* Porter or *Rosa caroliniana* Michx.	Sarah Everett	Osowatomie area
Prickly Pear	Plains Prickly-pear	*Opuntia macrorhiza* Engelm.	Miriam Colt	Neosho R., Allen Co.
Scarlet Milkweed	Butterfly Milkweed	*Asclepias tuberosa* L.	Lucy Carruth	Osawatomie area
Sensitive plant	Catclaw Sensitive-briar	*Mimosa nuttallii* (DC.) B. L. Turner	Miriam Colt	Neosho R, Allen Co.
			Mary Sears	Hesper, Douglas Co.
Snakes Head	False Dragonhead	*Physostegia angustifolia* Fernald	Miriam Colt	Neosho R., Allen Co.
Spiderwort	Spiderwort	*Tradescantia ohiensis* Raf.	Miriam Colt	Neosho R., Allen Co.
			Lucy Carruth	Osawatomie area
Spring Beauty	Spring Beauty	*Claytonia virginica* L.	Sarah Everett	Osawatomie area
Sweet Pea	Hoary Peavine	*Lathyrus polymorphus* Nutt.	Mary Sears	Hesper, Douglas Co.
Sweet William	Sweet-William Phlox	*Phlox divaricata* L. subsp. *laphamii* Wherry	Miriam Colt	Neosho R., Allen Co.
			Sarah Everett	Osawatomie area
Wild hops	Common Hops	*Humulus lupulus* L.	Charles Lines	15 miles SSE of Manhattan (Wabaunsee)
Wild Sorrel / Sheep Sorrel	Violet Wood Sorrel	*Oxalis violacea* L.	Sarah Everett	Osawatomie area

Writer's Reference	Common Name (possible)	Scientific Name	Writer	Location
Wild Strawberry	Wild Strawberry	*Fragaria virginiana* Mill.	Charles Lines	15 miles SSE of Manhattan (Wabaunsee)
			John Stillman Brown	Lawrence
Yellow star-like thing	Yellow Stargrass	*Hypoxis hirsuta* (L.) Coville	Sarah Everett	Osawatomie area
GRASSES				
Grama	Side-Oats Grama	*Bouteloua curtipendula* (Michx.) Torr.	George Walter	SW part of Territory
WOODY PLANTS				
Ash	Green Ash	*Fraxinus pennsylvanica* Marshall	George Walter	Not specified
Bass	American Basswood	*Tilia americana* L.	George Walter	Not specified
Birch	River Birch	*Betula nigra* L.	George Walter	Not specified
Black Walnut	Black Walnut	*Juglans nigra* L.	George Walter	Not specified
			Robert Tovey	Osawatomie area
			Moses C. Sessions	Centerville, Linn Co.
			Walter Woods	Sumner, Atchison Co.
Boxelder	Boxelder	*Acer negundo* L.	Joseph Trego	Sugar Mound (now Mound City), Linn Co.
Bur Oak	Bur Oak	*Quercus macrocarpa*	Robert Tovey	Osawatomie area
Coffee Bean	Kentucky Coffeetree	*Gymnocladus dioicus* (L.) K. Koch	George Walter	Not specified
Cottonwood	Eastern Cottonwood	*Populus deltoides* W. Bartram ex Marshall	George Walter	Not specified
			Robert Tovey	Osawatomie area
Crab Apple	Wild Crabapple	*Malus ioensis* (Alph. Wood) Britton	George Walter	Not specified
Elm	American Elm	*Ulmus americana* L.	George Walter	Not specified
			Moses C. Sessions	Centerville, Linn Co.
Gooseberry	Gooseberry	*Ribes missouriense* Nutt.	Lucy Carruth	Osawatomie area
			George Walter	Not specified
			John Stillman Brown	Lawrence
Grapes	Riverbank Grape	*Vitis riparia* Michx.	Charles Lines	15 Miles SSE of Manhattan (Wabaunsee)
			Thomas Wells	Manhattan
			John Stillman Brown	Lawrence

Writer's Reference	Common Name (possible)	Scientific Name	Writer	Location
Hackberry	Hackberry	*Celtis occidentalis* L.	Moses C. Sessions Robert Tovey	Centerville, Linn Co. Osawatomie area
Horse Chestnut	Western Buckeye	*Aesculus glabra* Willd.	Joseph Trego	Sugar Mound (now Mound City), Linn Co.
Locust	Honeylocust	*Gleditsia triacanthos* L.	George Walter C. B. Boynton	Not specified Various areas
Mulberry	Red Mulberry	*Morus rubra* L.	Joseph Trego George Walter John Stillman Brown	Sugar Mound (now Mound City), Linn Co. Not specified Lawrence
Pawpaw	Pawpaw	*Asimina triloba* (L.) Dunal	George Walter Walter Woods	Not specified Sumner, Atchison Co.
Pecan	Pecan	*Carya illinoinensis* (Wangenh.) K. Koch	Melissa Genett Anderson	Neosho R., Allen Co.
Persimmon	Persimmon	*Diospyros virginiana* L.	George Walter Melissa Genett Anderson	Not specified Neosho R., Allen Co.
Plum	Plum	*Prunus americana* Marshall	Joseph Trego Thomas Wells	Sugar Mound (now Mound City), Linn Co. Manhattan
Raspberry	Black Raspberry	*Rubus occidentalis* L.	Lucy Carruth Samuel J. Reader	Osawatomie area Indianola, Butler Co.
Red Cedar	Eastern Red Cedar	*Juniperus virginiana* L.	George Walter	Not specified
Sassafras	Sassafras	*Sassafras albidum* (Nutt.) Nees	George Walter	Not specified
Shellbark Hickory	Shellbark Hickory	*Carya laciniosa* (F. Michx.) Loudon	George Walter	Not specified
Slippery Elm	Red Elm	*Ulmus rubra* Muhl.	Robert Tovey C. B. Boynton	Osawatomie area Various areas
Sugar Tree	Sugar Maple	*Acer saccharum* Marshall	Joseph Trego Robert Tovey	Sugar Mound (now Mound City), Linn Co. Osawatomie area
Sycamore	American Sycamore	*Platanus occidentalis* L.	George Walter Moses C. Sessions Robert Tovey	Not specified Centerville, Linn Co. Osawatomie area
White Oak	White Oak	Quercus alba L.	C. B. Boynton	Various areas
Wild Cherry	Wild Cherry	Prunus sp.	George Walter	Not specified

Many of the plant determinations listed are conjecture based on the limited information available—i.e., plant description, flowering/fruiting time, and location.

BIBLIOGRAPHY

Adair, Samuel Lyle. Diary. Samuel and Fiorella Adair Collection, Kansas State Historical Society, Territorial Kansas Online (www.territorialkansasonline .org). Item No. 100575. Accessed October 2, 2012.

———. Record of Marriages. Samuel and Fiorella Adair Collection, Kansas State Historical Society, Territorial Kansas Online (www.territorialkansasonline .org). Item No. 100577. Accessed November 4, 2006.

Allen, Chestina Bowker. Sketches and Journal, History of Pottawatomie County. Kansas State Historical Society, Territorial Kansas Online (www .territorialkansasonline.org). Item No. 102802. Accessed November 4, 2006.

Anderson, Melissa Genett. The Story of a Kansas Pioneer. Mt. Vernon, OH: The Manufacturing Printers Co., 1924.

Bacon, L. S. Diary. Manuscript Collections, Kansas State Historical Society, Topeka.

Barclay's Business Directory of Leavenworth. Leavenworth: Frank P. Barclay's English, French and German Printing Establishment, 1859.

Barnes, Lela, ed. "Letters of Cyrus Kurtz Holliday," Kansas Historical Quarterly 6 (August 1937), 241–294.

Bayless, John. John Bayless to Mrs. C. J. Minion, 14 January 1856. University of Kansas, Territorial Kansas Online (www.territorialkansasonline.org). Item No. 102109. Accessed October 12, 2006.

Bemeking, Carolyn. "A Look at Early Lawrence, Letters from Robert Gaston Elliott," Kansas Historical Quarterly 43 (Autumn 1977), 282–296.

Benefit Ball Invitation. Kansas State Historical Society, Territorial Kansas Online (www.territorialkansasonline.org). Item No. 102577. Accessed October 6, 2004.

Blackmar, Frank W., ed. Kansas: A Cyclopedia of State History, Embracing Events, Institutions, Industries, Counties, Cities, Towns, Prominent Persons, Etc. 2 vols. Chicago: Standard Publishing Co., 1912.

Bourassa, Joseph N. Joseph N. Bourassa (Ke Kahn) to Thomas Stenson, 6 September 1856. Thomas Nesbit Stenson Collection, Kansas State Historical Society, Territorial Kansas Online (www.territorialkansasonline.org). Item No. 100220. Accessed November 10, 2012.

——. Joseph N. Bourassa (Ke Kahn) to Thomas Stenson, 29 December 1856. Thomas Nesbit Stenson Collection, Kansas State Historical Society, Territorial Kansas Online (www.territorialkansasonline.org). Item No. 100251. Accessed November 4, 2006.

Boynton, Rev. C. B., and T. B. Mason. *Journey through Kansas.* Cincinnati: Moore, Wilstach, Keys and Company, 1855.

Brinkerhoff, Fred W. "The Kansas Tour of Lincoln the Candidate," *Kansas Historical Quarterly* 13 (February 1945), 286–309.

Brown, John Stillman. John Stillman Brown to William Brown, 21 June 1857. John Stillman Brown Collection, Kansas State Historical Society, Territorial Kansas Online (www.territorialkansasonline.org). Item No. 101717. Accessed November 4, 2006.

Burlington (KS) *Independent.* Obituaries, December 25, 1896.

Carruth, Lucy, and Jane Carruth. Letters. Manuscript Collection, Kansas State Historical Society, Topeka.

Cather, Willa. *O, Pioneers!* New York: Barnes & Noble Classics, 2003 (first published 1913, Houghton Mifflin Co.).

Chapman, J. Butler. *The History of Kansas and Emigrant's Guide.* Akron: Teesdale, Elkins and Co., 1855.

Clark, Shelly Hickman and James W. Clark, eds., "Lawrence in 1854: The Recollections of Joseph Savage," *Kansas History* 27 (Spring–Summer 2004), 30–43.

Colt, Miriam. *Went to Kansas.* Watertown, NY: L. Ingalls and Co., 1862.

Connelley, William E. *A Standard History of Kansas and Kansans.* 5 vols. Chicago: Lewis Publishing Co., 1919.

Cordley, Richard. "The Convention Epoch in Kansas History," *Transactions of the Kansas State Historical Society,* V (1889–1896), 42–47.

——. *Pioneer Days in Kansas.* Boston: Pilgrim Press, 1903.

Cutler, William G. *History of the State of Kansas.* Chicago: A.T. Andreas, 1883.

Deering, John H. Diary. Kansas State Historical Society, Topeka.

Denison, Henry. Isaac Goodnow Collection, Kansas State Historical Society, Territorial Kansas Online (www.territorialkansasonline.org). Item No. 102388. Accessed October 30, 2010.

(Emporia) *Kanzas News.* "The Crops," June 20, 1857.

——. "Buckwheat," July 4, 1857.

——. "Loafers Club," July 25, 1857.

———. "Emigration," August 1, 1857.

———. "Lecture on Kansas," September 19, 1857.

———. "Emigration," September 26, 1857.

Etcheson, Nicole. "The Great Principle of Self-Government: Popular Sovereignty and Bleeding Kansas," in Dean, *Kansas Territorial Reader*. Topeka, KS: 2005. 53–67.

Everett, John, and Sarah Everett. "Letters of John and Sarah Everett, 1854–1864," Pts. 1 & 2, *Kansas Historical Quarterly* 8 (February 1939): 3–34, 8; (May 1939): 143–174.

Fletcher, J. M. "Sleighing," *(Topeka) Kansas Tribune,* March 10, 1859.

Gilbert, Robert. Autobiography. University of Kansas, Territorial Kansas Online (www.territorialkansasonline.org). Item No. 101594. Accessed October 30, 2012.

Giles, F. W. *Thirty Years in Topeka.* Topeka, KS: Geo. W. Crane and Co., 1886.

Goodlander, C. W. *Memoirs and Recollections of C. W. Goodlander of Early Days of Fort Scott.* Fort Scott, KS: Monitor Book and Printing Co., 1899.

Goodnow, Ellen. Ellen Goodnow to Harriet Goodnow, 18 May 1856. Isaac Goodnow Collection, Kansas State Historical Society, Territorial Kansas Online (www.territorialkansasonline.org). Item No. 102332. Accessed February 25, 2006.

Goodnow, Isaac. Isaac Goodnow to Eli Thayer, 24 May 1858. Eli Thayer Collection, Kansas State Historical Society, Territorial Kansas Online (www .territorialkansasonline.org). Item No. 102370. Accessed November 3, 2011.

———. Diary. Isaac Goodnow Collection, Kansas State Historical Society, Topeka.

Goodnow, William E. William Goodnow to Harriet Goodnow, 10 June 1855. Isaac Goodnow Collection, Kansas Historical Society, Territorial Kansas Online (www.territorialkansasonline.org). Item No. 102320. Accessed May 15, 2012.

Green, C. R. *Green's Historical Series.* Vol. 1, *Early Days in Kansas: Along the Santa Fe Trail in the Counties of Douglas, Franklin, Shawnee, Osage, and Lyon.* Olathe: C. R. Green, 1912.

Griffing, James Sayre. James Sayre Griffing to J. Augusta Goodrich Griffing, 7 August 1859. James Sayre Griffing Collection, Kansas Historical Society, Territorial Kansas Online (www.territorialkansasonline.org). Item No. 102898. Accessed September 9, 2011.

Griffing, William. "Private Letters—The Correspondence of James S. Griffing and J. Augusta Goodrich" (www.griffingweb.com). Accessed May 13, 2010.

Hildt, George. "The Diary of George Hildt," *Kansas Historical Quarterly* 10 (August 1941), 260–298.

Holder, C. W. C. W. Holder to James Blood, 27 October 1860. James Blood Collection, Kansas State Historical Society, Territorial Kansas Online (www .territorialkansasonline.org). Item No. 101297. Accessed May 30, 2012.

Holliday, Cyrus Kurtz. Cyrus K. Holliday to Mary Holliday, 3 December 1854. Cyrus Kurtz Holliday Collection, Kansas State Historical Society, Territorial Kansas Online (www.territorialkansasonline.org). Item No. 101435. Accessed November 6, 2010.

———. Cyrus K. Holliday to Mary Holliday, 7 January 1855. Cyrus Kurtz Holliday Collection, Kansas State Historical Society, Territorial Kansas Online (www .territorialkansasonline.org). Item No. 101459. Accessed August 25, 2012.

Hoole, William Stanley, ed. "A Southerner's Viewpoint of the Kansas Situation," Pt. 1, *Kansas Historical Quarterly* 3 (February 1934), 43–56.

Hubbell, Willard Orvis. Diary. Kansas State Historical Society, Territorial Kansas Online (www.territorialkansasonline.org). Item No. 100207. Accessed November 6, 2006.

Ingalls, John James. John James Ingalls to Elias T. Ingalls, 2 December 1858. John James Ingalls Collection, Kansas State Historical Society, Territorial Kansas Online (www.territorialkansasonline.org). Item No. 102034. Accessed January 12, 2012.

———. John James Ingalls to Elias T. Ingalls, 21 August 1860. John James Ingalls Collection, Kansas State Historical Society, Territorial Kansas Online (www .territorialkansasonline.org). Item No. 102030. Accessed January 12, 2012.

"John Greenleaf Whittier," *Transactions of the Kansas State Historical Society*, 5 (1889–1896), 30.

Kansas History and Heritage Project, Riley County, Kansas (www.rootsweb .ancestry.com/-ksriley/index.html). Accessed June 5, 2012.

Kansas Philomathic Institute. *The Prairie Star.* Samuel E. Martin Collection, Kansas State Historical Society, Territorial Kansas Online (www .territorialkansasonline.org). Item No. 100193. Accessed November 4, 2006.

KSGenWeb Project (http://skyways.lib.ks.us/genweb).

Ladies of Orange, New Jersey. Ladies of Orange, New Jersey, to Thaddeus Hyatt, 20 October 1856. Thaddeus Hyatt Collection, Kansas State Historical Society, Territorial Kansas Online (www.territorialkansasonline.org). Item No. 101449. Accessed August 1, 2010.

(Lawrence, KS) *Democrat Journal*. "Horticultural Meeting," June 22, 1906.

(Lawrence, KS) *Herald of Freedom*. "New Year's Supper," January 6, 1855.

———. "Cotton Cloth," January 13, 1855.

———. "A Crowd in the Spring," January 13, 1855.

———. "Kansas Athenaeum," January 13, 1855.

———. "Sabbath School," January 13, 1855.

———. "Topeka," January 13, 1855.

———. "Free Day School," January 20, 1855.

———. "Book for the Athenaeum," January 27, 1855.

———. "Let's All Go to Kansas," January 27, 1855.

———. Advertisement, January 24, 1857.

———. "The Church Going Bell," April 25, 1857.

———. "The New England Bards," July 18, 1857.

———. "Lawrence Sewing Circle," August 8, 1857.

———. "After a Shower," August 10, 1857.

———. "Clothing for Kansas," August 10, 1857.

———. "The Lawrence Cornet Band," September 12, 1857.

———. "Promenade Concert," September 19, 1857.

———. "The Weather," September 19, 1857.

———. "Sewing Societies," January 9, 1858.

(Lawrence) *Kansas Tribune*. "Hope," May 23, 1855.

———. "Some Pumpkins," October 17, 1855.

Litchfield, Timothy. Diary. Timothy Lewis Litchfield Collection, RH VLT MS B6. Kenneth Spencer Research Library, University of Kansas Libraries, Lawrence.

Lovejoy, Julia Louisa. Diary. Charles and Julia Lovejoy Collection, Kansas State Historical Society, Topeka.

———. "Letters from Kansas," Pt. 1, *Kansas Historical Quarterly* 11 (February 1942), 29–44.

MacLean, Maggie. "Poets and Writers," Civil War Women Blog (www.civilwarwomenblog.com). Accessed October 2, 2012.

Mayo, Elisha Frank. Thankful Sophia Mayo journal, Kansas Collection, Kenneth Spencer Research Library, University of Kansas Libraries, Lawrence.

Mayo, Thankful Sophia. Journal. Kansas Collection, RH MS E191, Kenneth Spencer Research Library, University of Kansas Libraries, Lawrence.

McVicar, Peter. Peter McVicar Collection, Kansas State Historical Society, Territorial Kansas Online (www.territorialkansasonline.org). Item No. 100246. Accessed November 7, 2011.

Mead, James R. James R. Mead to Mother, 25 December 1860. James Mead Collection, Kansas State Historical Society, Territorial Kansas Online (www.territorialkansasonline.org). Item No. 101963. Accessed November 4, 2006.

Miller, Joseph C. Diary. Manuscript Collection, Kansas State Historical Society, Topeka.

Murray, Donald M., and Robert M. Rodney, eds. "The Letters of Peter Bryant, Jackson County Pioneer," *Kansas Historical Quarterly* 27 (Autumn 1961), 320–352.

New Year's Hop Invitation. Kansas State Historical Society, Territorial Kansas Online (www.territorialkansasonline.org). Item No. 102573. Accessed February 25, 2006.

Prantle, Alberta, ed. "The Connecticut Kansas Colony; Letters of Charles B. Lines to the New Haven (Conn.) Daily Palladium," *Kansas Historical Quarterly* 22 (Spring 1956), 1–50.

Peterson, John M., ed. "The Letters of Edward and Sarah Fitch, 1855–1863," Pt. 1, *Kansas History* 12 (Spring 1989), 48–70.

———. "The Letters of Edward and Sarah Fitch, 1855–1863," Pt. 2, *Kansas History* 12 (Summer 1989): 78–100.

———. "The Letters of Edward and Sarah Fitch, 1855–1863," Pt. 2, *Kansas History* 20 (Summer 1997): 68–85.

Puffer, Charles. Diary. Manuscript Collections, Kansas State Historical Society, Topeka.

Randolph, Anna Margaret. Diary. Anna Margaret Watson Randolph Collection, Kansas State Historical Society, Topeka.

Reader, Samuel James. Diary. Samuel James Reader Collection, Kansas State Historical Society, Territorial Kansas Online (www.territorialkansasonline.org). Item No. 100375. Accessed November 24, 2006.

Robinson, Sara T. L. *Kansas: Its Interior and Exterior Life.* Boston: Crosby, Nichols and Co., 1856.

Ropes, Hannah Anderson. *Six Months in Kansas.* Boston: John P. Jewett and Co., 1856.

Russcll, Marian. *Land of Enchantment*. Evanston: Branding Iron Press, 1954. Reprinted with an afterword by Marc Simmons. Albuquerque: University of New Mexico Press, 1981.

Sears, Mary A., William Henry Sears, and L. William Thavis. *Pioneering in Kansas: Iowa to Kansas in an Ox Wagon; Experiences of Capt. Charles M. Sears and Family in the '50s*. Washington, DC: Kansas State Society, 1917.

Sessions, Moses C. Moses C. Sessions to Sir, 10 January 1858. Kansas State Historical Society, Territorial Kansas Online (www.territorialkansasonline .org). Item No. 102451. Accessed September 23, 2006.

Stewart, James R. "The Diary of James R. Stewart, Pioneer of Osage County," Pt. 1, *Kansas Historical Quarterly* 17 (February 1949), 1–36.

Tomlinson, William P. *Kansas in Eighteen Fifty-Eight*. New York: H. Dayton. 1859.

(Topeka) *Kansas Tribune*. "The Anniversary of the Philomathic Institute," January 5, 1857.

———. "Philomathic Institute," February 2, 1857.

———. "Philomathic Institute," February 15, 1857.

———. "Plant Trees," April 6, 1857.

———. "The Christmas Party," December 26, 1857.

———. "The Drama," March 27, 1858.

———. "New England Bards," May 29, 1858.

———. "Topeka Dramatic Company," May 29, 1858.

———. "New Year's at Brownville," December 16, 1858.

———. "Sleighing," December 16, 1858.

———. Advertisement, December 23, 1858.

———. "Holiday Festivals," January 1, 1859.

———. "Philomathic Institute," February 10, 1859.

———. "Emigration," March 24, 1859.

———. "May Party," May 12, 1859.

———. "Lectures," June 2, 1859.

———. Advertisement, June 23, 1859.

———. "The Show," July 7, 1859.

———. "Mabie's Circus," July 14, 1859.

Tovey, Robert Atkins. Robert Atkins Tovey, Sr. Collection, Kenneth Spencer Research Library, University of Kansas Libraries, Lawrence.

Trego, Joseph Harrington. Joseph Harrington Trego Collection, Kansas State Historical Society, Territorial Kansas Online (www.territorialkansasonline .org). Item Nos. 101260, 102618, 102619, 102620. Accessed November 4, 2006.

Tucker, Edwin. Diary. Manuscript Collection, Kansas State Historical Society, Topeka.

US Bureau of the Census. Kansas State Census Collection, 1855–1925. US Bureau of the Census, Washington, D.C.

US Congress. Biographical Directory (bioguide.congress.gov). Accessed January 12, 2012.

Valentine, Daniel Mulford. Diary. Kansas State Historical Society, Territorial Kansas Online (www.territorialkansasonline.org). Item No. 103090. Accessed November 11, 2006.

Walter, George. *History of Kanzas, Also Information Regarding Routes, Laws, Etc.* Kansas State Historical Society, Territorial Kansas Online (www .territorialkansasonline.org). Item No. 102640. Accessed November 4, 2006.

Washington's Birthday Ball Invitation. Kansas State Historical Society, Territorial Kansas Online (www.territorialkansasonline.org). Item No. 102572. Accessed November 4, 2006.

Wells, Thomas C. "Letters of a Kansas Pioneer," Pt. 1, *Kansas Historical Quarterly* 5 (May 1936), 143–179.

———. "Letters of a Kansas Pioneer," Pt. 2, *Kansas Historical Quarterly* 5 (August 1936), 282–313.

Whitman, E. B. Expense sheet. Thaddeus Hyatt Collection, Kansas State Historical Society, Topeka.

Whitney, E. S. E. S. Whitney to Hiram Hill, 20 August 1856. Hiram Hill Collection, Kansas State Historical Society, Territorial Kansas Online (www .territorialkansasonline.org). Item No. 102157. Accessed October 26, 2011.

Whittier, J. G. "The Kansas Emigrant Song," Lyric sheet. Kansas State Historical Society, Territorial Kansas Online (www.territorialkansasonline.org). Item No. 100658. Accessed November 4, 2006.

Wilmarth, Otis. Advertisement calendar, Kansas State Historical Society, Territorial Kansas Online (www.territorialkansasonline.org). Item No. 102751. Accessed November 11, 2006.

Woods, Walter Hastings. Diary. Manuscript Collection, Kansas State Historical Society, Topeka.

INDEX

A

Adair, Fiorella, 76
Adair, Reverence Samuel, 75–77, 113, 183–84
Alcott, Louisa May, 130
Allen, Asahel Gilbert, 26
Allen, Chestina Bowker, 26–27, 32
American Home Missionary Society, 116
American Reform Tract and Book Society, 108
Ancient Free and Accepted Masons, 3, 30, 32
Anderson, Hannah, 129–30
Anderson, Melissa Genett, 80–81, 114, 118, 119–20, 167, 168
"Andover Band," 116,
animals, 47, 61–63, 81, 154–57
apples, 59, 71, 94
"Astor House," 98
Atchison, Kansas, 93
Atchison, Topeka, and the Santa Fe Railroad, 101
Athenaeum, 165–66

B

Bacon, Ellen Moor, 128
Bacon, Lewis S., 95, 128
Baker University, 4
Barclay's Business Directory of Leavenworth, 2
Bayless, John, 148–49
Benes, Eleanor, 125
birds, 156–57
Bishop, Mary E., 77
Blood, James, 95, 144
Bluemont College, 4, 22, 24
bookstore, 33, 159
Bourassa, Joseph N., 171–72
Boynton, Charles B., 108, 115
Brown, John Stillman, 47, 57–58, 91
Brown, Mary Ripley, 57
Bryant, Peter, 94, 125, 126–27
buckwheat, 47, 59

C

"Candy Manufactory," 144
Carruth, James Harrison, 52
Carruth, Jane, 47, 52, 90
Carruth, Lucy, 52–53
celebrations, 23, 47, 69–81, 121–27, 146, 168–77

ABOUT THE EDITOR AND ILLUSTRATOR

Linda Johnston began reading pioneer diaries in 1986 and never stopped. Though her own emigration to Kansas came 140 years after the accounts included in this book, she understood the settlers' apprehension about leaving home and friends for an unfamiliar place. Extensive archival research enabled her to present these writings in their historical context and to bring them into conversation with one another. Her background as an artist and naturalist gives a unique perspective on these sixty remarkable individuals who wrote not only of their hardships and challenges, but their joys as well. Linda now lives in northern Virginia with her husband, Clay.